W9-ALX-418

CLEOPATRA
RULER OF EGYPT

1/2008

CLEOPATRA
RULER OF EGYPT

Kerrily Sapet

MORGAN
REYNOLDS
PUBLISHING
Greensboro, North Carolina

CLEOPATRA: RULER OF EGYPT

Copyright © 2007 by Kerrily Sapet

Library of Congress Cataloging-in-Publication Data

Sapet, Kerrily, 1972-
    Cleopatra : ruler of Egypt / by Kerrily Sapet. -- 1st ed.
      p. cm.
    Includes bibliographical references and index.
    ISBN-13: 978-1-59935-035-6
    ISBN-10: 1-59935-035-1
    1. Cleopatra, Queen of Egypt, d. 30 B.C. 2. Egypt--History--332-30 B.C.
3. Rome--History--Civil War, 43-31 B.C. 4. Queens--Egypt--Biography.
I. Title.
    DT92.7.S27 2007
    932'.021092--dc22
    [B]

                            2006033381

Printed in the United States of America
First Edition

To my sisters, who like the Queen of the Nile,
are both beautiful and courageous

Contents

A Note on Sources

There is very little primary historical documentation about the life of Cleopatra. Most of what we know comes from histories written by Romans after her death. These accounts are often suspect because many were written during the reign of her archenemy Augustus Caesar and by men who were often under his patronage.

This book tries to weigh the sources, to evaluate any biases, and to supplement these accounts with the discoveries made by later historians and others who have studied the ancient world. It attempts to provide as balanced and accurate an account of her life as possible while remembering that no historical record is ever definitive or complete.

In the words of Plutarch:

It is so hard to find out the truth of anything by looking at the record of the past. The process of time obscures the truth of former times, and even contemporaneous writers disguise and twist the truth out of malice or flattery.

Cleopatra

one

THE SEVENTH CLEOPATRA

According to one Egyptian myth, the Nile River was born out of the profound grief of Isis, the powerful goddess of fertility and rebirth. In this creation story, when Osiris, Isis's husband, who was also her brother, was murdered by his brother Set, his body was severed into thirteen pieces that Set scattered throughout Egypt. After the murder, the grief stricken Isis spent years searching for her dead husband's parts, weeping the entire time, until her tears formed the four-thousand-mile-long Nile River.

Isis was finally able to find twelve of Osiris's thirteen pieces and, after casting a magic spell on the disjointed limbs, was able to bring him back to life for a single night, during which the couple conceived their son, Horus. Osiris, after his brief resurrection, went on to become the god of the dead and the underworld and Horus became the god of the sun and the sky, and the Nile River spawned ancient Egyptian civilization.

The story of Isis and Osiris was one of the central myths in Egypt for centuries. In addition to explaining the creation of the life-giving Nile, it also helped establish and justify the tradition of the

The story of Isis and Osiris became one of the central myths in the Egyptian religion.

ruling pharaoh marrying a sibling as a way to keep the ruling family's blood pure. Pharaohs defined themselves as incarnations of the gods, giving their rules divine justification. Cleopatra, one of Egypt's most famous and influential queens, depicted herself as Isis, and her story is just as dramatic as the myth.

Cleopatra was born in late 70 or early 69 B.C. Her father, King Ptolemy XII, was one of the last in a long line of kings who, according to tradition, had renamed themselves Ptolemy when they assumed the throne of Egypt. Most historians believe that Cleopatra's mother was Cleopatra V Tryphene, Ptolemy XII's first wife and, following the

This rendition of Horus with 'Shen rings' in his grasp hangs in the Louvre Museum in Paris.

pharonic tradition, also his sister. Little is known about her except that she died shortly after giving birth to Cleopatra, her third daughter. The Ptolemaic kings and queens named their daughters either Berenice, Arsinoë, or Cleopatra, which means "glory of her father" in Greek.

When Cleopatra was an infant, her father married a woman whose name is lost. Within ten years, Cleopatra had a younger half-sister, Arsinoë IV, and two younger half-brothers, Ptolemy XIII and Ptolemy XIV. She also had two older sisters, Cleopatra VI and Berenice IV. Sandwiched between older siblings and younger half-siblings, it was unlikely that she would ever rule Egypt, one of the wealthiest realms in the ancient world.

Located in northeastern Africa, most of Cleopatra's Egypt was covered by desert that ancient Egyptians called the *de-shret*, meaning "red lands." Although the vast, arid desert could not support a large population, Egyptians believed their land was blessed by the gods because of the Nile. The world's longest river, the Nile flows north through its delta until it empties into the Mediterranean Sea, nourishing a fertile valley in the midst of the desert.

Each year in August, the Nile swelled from the monsoon rains that fell in the highlands of Ethopia until it overflowed its banks. When the river's floodwaters receded in October, they left behind deposits of sticky, black mud spread across the floodplain. The Egyptians called these rich areas the *kemet* or "black lands." Farmers sowed their crops in this rich soil. Golden wheat,

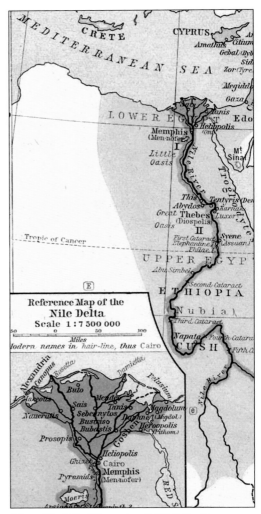

Map of the Nile River, circa 1450 B.C. At 4,165 miles long, the world's longest river flows from south to north to empty into the Mediterranean Sea.

amber barley, fruits, and vegetables grew quickly in the hot sun. Exported across the known world, these grains and other products made Egypt rich. To increase food production the industrious Egyptians also developed new

For centuries, the land of Egypt has depended on the seasonal flooding of the Nile River to enrich the soil. (Courtesy of the Associated Press)

farming techniques, such as irrigation systems and the use of plows, rakes, and fertilizers made from manure.

Along with fertile soil, the vast river offered other benefits. Fish and waterfowl lived in and around the water, and two important plants, flax and papyrus, grew on the river's banks. Flax was used to weave fine linen cloth, and papyrus was used in the making of boats, rope, baskets, and, most importantly, an early form of paper.

Cutting long strips of the inner papyrus plant, the Egyptians pounded and soaked the strips for three days. They then wove the strips together and pressed them between cotton sheets to remove the moisture. The resultant lightweight, durable writing material revolutionized record keeping and literature. Because the Egyptians kept their

Papyrus and flax

manufacturing methods secret from the outside world, papyrus became an almost exclusively Egyptian commodity.

For more than eight thousand years before Cleopatra's birth, Egyptian civilization developed and flourished along the banks of the Nile. Pharaohs, ruled these "red and black lands," building magnificent palaces and temples on the east bank of the river. This bank, above which the sun rose, was known traditionally as the land of the living. They built towering pyramid tombs on the river's west bank, or the land of the dead, where the sun set. The carefully mummified remains of the pharaohs lay in these royal tombs, surrounded by art and possessions they would need in the afterlife. Bold red, yellow, blue, and black hiero-glyphics were written on the walls around them, relating the stories of their lives and rule. Worshiped as gods by their people, the pharaohs united northern and southern Egypt into one kingdom.

The pharaoh was the pinnacle of Egyptian society and ruled over layers of bureaucracy composed of edu-cated Egyptian officials, nobles, priests, and commoners. The pharaoh controlled tremendous resources. All of Egypt was his property. He was the supreme warlord, the chief priest of every god, and the head of the civil

Example of hieroglyphic writing of the 19th dynasty on the Tomb of Sehti I in the Valley of the Kings. (Courtesy of Giraudon /Art Resource)

administration. Considered to be both worldly and divine, the pharaoh oversaw everything from legal disputes to religious rites—it was his responsibility to satisfy the gods by making sacrifices and offerings so they would bless Egypt with the Nile's bountiful flood.

Egypt survived and evolved for thousands of years under various dynasties until 332 B.C., when it was conquered

Egyptian Pharaohs were buried in elaborate tombs inside the pyramids. (Courtesy of the Associated Press)

by Alexander the Great. Alexander was from Macedonia, a kingdom in northern Greece. Following in his father Philip's footsteps, Alexander seized control of the quarreling Greek city states, then turned his attention to the East. Eventually, Alexander and his armies conquered the once mighty Persians, and took Egypt and the vast expanses of Central Asia all the way to present-day India. In the process, Alexander and his army brought the culture that had been developing in Athens and the other Greek cities throughout the Mediterranean region into southwestern Asia. The resultant fusion of Greek and Eastern culture

ABOVE: Philip, Alexander the Great's father (Courtesy of Alinari/Art Resource)

RIGHT: Alexander the Great (Courtesy of Scala /Art Resource)

and traditions that developed after Alexander has come to be known as Hellenistic civilization.

Alexander founded a new port city in Egypt on the Mediterranean Sea, west of the Nile River delta. In this new city of Alexandria, trade caravans from the East met Greek ships. It soon became one of the busiest ports in the Mediterranean region, a hub of the trade routes that traversed Europe and Africa and eastward to Arabia, China, and India. It also became the new capital of the Greek-ruled kingdom of Egypt.

When Alexander died in 323 B.C., his empire was parceled out among several of his generals. One of the generals, a distant cousin of Alexander's named Ptolemy, assumed control of Egypt, first as regent for the king's brother and infant son and then in his own right. Ptolemy kept and displayed Alexander's body in Alexandria, to lend legitimacy to his newfound authority. Over the next several decades, Ptolemy successfully defended his claim to the Egyptian throne as the entire Mediterranean region was engulfed in a series of wars over Alexander's territories known as the Wars of the Diadochi.

The Eastern Mediterranean in 90 B.C.

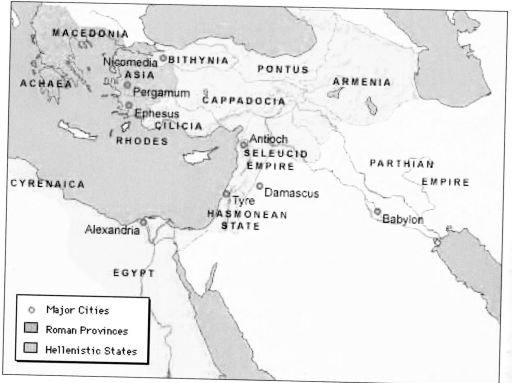

A romanticized portrait of Alexander fighting on his trusted horse, Bucephalus. (Courtesy of The Granger Collection)

In spite of his Macedonian heritage, Ptolemy thought it wise to claim to be a successor of the ancient pharaohs, and borrowed their symbols and rituals to win the support of the Egyptian people. He dressed simply, distinguishing himself only by wearing a *tainia*, a cloth headband considered to be a sacred symbol of royalty in Macedonia. Ptolemy, known as Ptolemy Soter ("Soter" means "savior"), founded the Ptolemaic dynasty in Egypt and worked to

A contemporary photo of the harbor at Alexandria, Egypt. The new library was built along the harbor only yards (meters) from where the 2,000-year-old original library is believed to have stood. (Courtesy of the Associated Press)

Bust of Ptolemy Soter as seen in the British Museum in London

expand his empire. By the time of Ptolemy III, Ptolemy I Soter's grandson, Egypt's vast holdings included Palestine, part of Syria, Cyrene (in modern day Libya), Cyprus, Crete, the Cyclades (a Greek island group in the Aegean Sea), numerous cities in Asia Minor (modern day Turkey), and distant Thrace (modern day Bulgaria).

The first Ptolemaic kings financed great festivities in the manner of the old pharaohs. Ptolemy II, known as Ptolemy Philadelphus, started the

Alexander the Great's empire stretched from Greece to the Indus Mountains. (Courtesy of North Wind Picture Archives)

Isolympic Games in Alexandria. Every four years, delegations from most of the Greek cities in the eastern Mediterranean met to compete in athletic events, horse races, and poetry and musical competitions. The second Ptolemaic pharaoh also restored an ancient maritime canal that the old pharaohs had built linking the Mediterranean Sea and the Red Sea at the port of Suez.

Alexandria formed the heart of the empire. The city exported wheat, African ebony and ivory, emeralds, amethysts, wool, linen, glassware, fruits, wines, valuable ostrich eggs, pottery, perfumes, metal goods, and papyrus scrolls, the writing material of scribes and scholars everywhere.

By the time of Cleopatra's birth, Alexandria was one of the wealthiest and most populous ports in the world. An estimated three million people lived in Egypt, and about half of them lived in the capital city. Cleopatra's ancestors ruled over an Alexandria that was the heart of most of the known world's technological, cultural and philosophical developments. It had a citywide public health system, the first of its kind, which strictly supervised hygiene and offered universal medical assistance. Drawn by the royal family's generous salaries, prominent Greek scholars journeyed to Alexandria where they enjoyed both prestige and wealth. Widely considered to be the most beautiful city in the world, Alexandria was home to the royal family's palace.

The royal palace in which Cleopatra spent her early years stood on the shores of Alexandria's eastern harbor. Unlike much of Egypt, which suffered through brutally hot summers, Alexandria was cooled by sea breezes. Marble and onyx columns lined the rooms of the palace, and long marble corridors led to rooms decorated in elaborate floor mosaics, wall paintings, and statues. Bedrooms had private baths and running water. Wide porches offered views overlooking the city, the harbor, and the nearby rocky islands where the royal family vacationed. The inner courtyards and surrounding gardens held fruit trees, fountains, and small ponds brimming with blue and white lotus blossoms.

Within the palace, the treasury room held Egypt's fortune in gold, precious stones, and jewelry. Hundreds of servants, palace guards, doctors, teachers, and cooks swarmed around the royal family. The palace's kitchens were busy at all hours with chefs preparing meats and sweet delicacies for the family and their guests.

Artist's rendition of Cleopatra's Palace (Courtesy of Bridgeman Art Library)

Cleopatra maintained her own sumptuous living quarters, where her servants bathed her in scented waters, served her superb foods, and dressed her in the finest linen and silk clothes. It was just a brief walk from the palace to Alexandria's other greatest treasures—its library and museum.

Although the Library of Alexandria was later destroyed, in Cleopatra's day it housed nearly seven hundred thousand papyrus scrolls, the world's largest collection. Construction of the library began under Ptolemy I Soter and was completed under Ptolemy II Philadelphus. Reputedly, Ptolemy Philadelphus amassed such a large collection by confiscating the scrolls of all visitors to the city, having scribes make copies by hand, returning the copies to the owners, and keeping the originals in the library's collection. Poets, writers, philosophers, mathematicians, astronomers, and doctors

The Library of Alexandria (Courtesy of North Wind Picture Archives)

Each of the nine Muses gave the gift of inspiration to a specific artform. (Courtesy of Giraudon /Art Resource)

collected, wrote, and stored the knowledge of the ancient world on these scrolls.

Next to the library was a temple dedicated to the nine Muses, the Greek goddesses who inspired artists and scientists, known as the "museum." Experts in philosophy, engineering, astronomy, geometry, geography, anatomy, medicine, language, and other branches of study gathered and exchanged ideas in the great hall and in its gardens, fountains, courtyards, and restaurants. Scholars did not pay taxes and were supported by the royal family. The king often required them to lay their research aside temporarily to fulfill his personal requests. He might set them to writing new poems in his praise, designing different richly colored cosmetics, creating genealogical trees, drawing maps, or building mechanical toys for festivals.

When not attending to the king's whims, the scholars made several significant discoveries. The Cyrenian-born Eratosthenes (276 B.C.–194 B.C.) was the first to determine the circumference of the Earth, which he did by measuring the sun's angle and the shadows it cast at different locations. Aristarchus (310 B.C.–230 B.C.) from Samos in Greece, was the first to postulate, almost eighteen centuries before Nicolas Copernicus, that the Earth revolved around the sun. Two physicians, Herophilus (335 B.C.–280 B.C.) and Erasistratus (330 B.C.–250 B.C.), identified the brain, rather than the heart, as the site of intelligence. Euclid (325 B.C.–265 B.C.), in his famous treatise, *The Elements*, laid out the foundations of geometry that would remain unchallenged until the nineteenth century. Wealthy Alexandrian children attended lectures by or received private tutoring from the world-renowned scholars in the museum's school.

Cleopatra's early education most likely took place amid the elegant marble halls, courtyards, and stacks of papyrus scrolls at the Alexandrian Library and Museum. Quick to learn, she absorbed mathematics, philosophy, medicine, and literature. She took lessons on the lyre, and practiced dancing, singing, drawing, and horseback riding. She heard and memorized the stories of the Greek and Egyptian gods and goddesses. As she grew older, she studied political science, examining the policies and tactics of earlier Greek and Egyptian rulers.

Cleopatra was particularly interested and adept in the study of foreign languages. By the time she was an adult, Cleopatra could speak Greek, Arabic, Hebrew, Ethiopic, Aramaic, Syriac, Parthian, Median, and the Roman language, Latin. She also learned Egyptian, which despite being the language of the people, was used infrequently by the Greek royal family.

One of Alexandria's glories was its lighthouse, the Pharos, named for the island in the city's harbor where it stood. Built during the reign of Ptolemy I Soter, the four-hundred-foot-tall lighthouse was topped with a glass lantern. A bright flame burned within it, day and night, reflected by mirrors visible far out at sea. The lighthouse welcomed ships to the safety of the city's deep harbor. Standing about 400 feet tall, the Pharos was one of the Seven Wonders of the Ancient World. Unfortunately the lighthouse crumbled over the centuries due to earthquakes, fires, and wars. Today, most of the island is under water.

Alexandria's famous Pharos lighthouse (Courtesy of The Granger Collection)

For recreation, residents of Alexandria attended a large amphitheater overlooking the city's harbor or played sports at a nearby gymnasium. The Greeks cherished physical training, believing it to be an important part of education. The Ptolemies also built a zoological garden that housed exotic animals. These public structures were built with colored polished stones and marble.

Other buildings, however, were built with more commonplace materials. Temples were fashioned of limestone and sandstone, while most homes were built with bricks. Workers molded the bricks from the Nile's silt and left them to dry in the sun rather than kiln-firing them. Only the most prestigious buildings and homes were made of more costly stone. By contrast, in Greece, workers were able to haul vast loads of white marble from nearby quarries. In Egypt, timber was also scarce.

Most Egyptians lived in small bungalows with attached courtyards. Living quarters and servants' rooms surrounded the courtyards. Entrances usually faced north in order to catch the Mediterranean breeze. Exterior windows were few, small, high, and usually covered by trellised screens made of wood and stone to keep out the heat and light of the sun. In luxurious homes the floors were paved with mosaics and decorations in the Greek style.

The pharaoh levied taxes to pay for the government, the army, and various rituals and ceremonies. Officials were paid in royal land grants. Priests composed a tiny, wealthy group of influential native elite. The Egyptian people, on whose labor the government and temples depended, lived in towns and villages grouped into units called nomes. The nomes were overseen by nomarchs, responsible for collecting the pharaoh's taxes and settling local disputes.

The pharaoh imposed strict controls on the Egyptian economy. Textiles, oil, and papyrus production were controlled by the state. Vast registries recorded the economic function and place of residence of every person in Egyptian society, from immigrant soldiers to peasants. Each year, villages were issued orders instructing which crops to plant. Peasants and animals were not allowed to leave during planting and harvesting seasons. "No one has the right to do what he wishes," proclaimed a Ptolemaic decree, "but everything is organized for the best."

Although Cleopatra's elegant lifestyle within the palace walls was very different from that of her father's subjects, it was far from carefree. Despite the privilege of being royalty, the seventh Cleopatra was largely alone. She had never known her mother, and her brothers and sisters were her rivals, not her friends. Young Cleopatra learned at an early age that her family members had murdered, poisoned, and stabbed their own relatives in order to advance to the throne. While in some kingdoms royal succession passed through the oldest son, in Egypt the pharaoh chose his successor. Her father would select from his six offspring. Cleopatra always needed to be on guard, watching her siblings, who were just as ambitious as she.

All of Cleopatra's siblings lived in their own apartments within the palace and kept their own staffs of servants and bodyguards. Losing the contest for power would most likely mean losing one's life. It was a struggle in which Cleopatra could not afford to trust anyone. Although she was guarded at all times, she was constantly followed by soldiers, servants, and guardians loyal to her scheming siblings. Just as they knew her plans, she made sure she knew theirs.

Life beyond the palace walls was just as dangerous. The Ptolemaic dynasty was much less powerful than it had been in previous generations. Starting with Ptolemy IV, the Ptolemaic pharaohs had grown increasingly greedy, weak, and corrupt. They lavishly spent state funds to build palaces in their own honor and to finance personal feuds. By the reign of Cleopatra's father, many of the dynasty's North African, Balkan, and Syrian territories had broken away.

Cleopatra's father, Ptolemy XII, abetted the decline through profligate spending. A foreign ambassador to the royal palace once observed eight enormous wild boars roasting before a banquet. He asked the royal chef how many people were expected to attend. The chef answered that there were only twelve guests and that they might only want wine. However, he was required at all times to have all sorts of dishes on hand in great quantities, just in case.

While the royal family lived in luxury, ordinary Alexandrians and the rest of Egypt suffered through droughts and famine. In years of scarce rain, when the Nile did not flood, fields were left dry and people starved. Conversely, excessive flooding could spread disease and kill livestock.

Ptolemy XII (Courtesy of Réunion des Musées Nationaux/Art Resource)

Dynastic struggles added to the chaos. As the pharaoh's children and wives plotted, their quarrels and conspiracies often spread to the streets, igniting civic unrest.

Seeing their rulers feasting and drinking, angry Alexandrians mocked them with ridiculous nicknames like *Physcon* (Ptolemy VIII's moniker, meaning "Fatty") or *Lathyrus* (Ptolemy IX's, meaning "Chickpea" because his nose was shaped like that legume). Cleopatra's father, Ptolemy XII, was derisively called *Auletes* or "the Flute Player" because of his habit of getting drunk and playing the flute. He once

Ptolemy IX (Courtesy of Bildarchiv Preussischer Kulturbesitz/Art Resource)

forced a courtier to drink wine until he was intoxicated, on pain of death, because the man never got drunk at Auletes's banquets. Auletes played his flute and danced in the streets during the festival of Dionysus, the Greek god of wine, arts, music, dancing, and drama, a spectacle that many Alexandrians considered to be undignified.

Although Auletes did repair many of the old buildings and temples of Egypt, he inspired little respect. More and more frequently the streets below the palace's porches seethed with violence as angry crowds fought with soldiers and guards.

Although they ruled Egypt, Cleopatra's family was Greek. Most Alexandrians were among the waves of Greek and Jewish settlers who had followed Alexander and Ptolemy I Soter into Egypt. Ultimately, they displaced almost all of the Egyptians in the army and the government.

A relief sculpture located in the Vatican Museum, Rome, representing Greek life.

Vast class differences divided the Greeks from the native Egyptians. Greeks dominated the Egyptians, most of whom survived by working the land. The Ptolemies granted Greek settlers large pastoral estates along the Nile, on which they cultivated wheat, grapes, and olives, and lorded over the Egyptian peasants who worked their lands. Egyptians were also forced to work on canals and dikes designed to make the land more productive for the wealthy landowners. Different legal systems and laws for Greeks, Egyptians, and Jews created constant tension. One Egyptian servant who worked for the Ptolemies complained that he had not been paid for months "because I am a barbarian." (The word "barbarian" was derived from the

Greek word *barbaroi*, which meant "someone who does not speak Greek.")

Over time, the strict divisions in Egyptian society began to relax. The privileged class expanded to include anyone who spoke Greek, adopted Greek lifestyles and names, and worshiped the Egyptian gods that had been given Greek names. Children of mixed marriages, Egyptians who received a Greek education, and Jews were all considered Greek as long as they spoke the language. Being considered Greek had many benefits. It made one eligible for higher-ranking government jobs, lower taxes, and exemptions from publicly humiliating punishments. Most upper-class Egyptians and Jews sought Greek identification through education.

While the story of Isis and Osiris established the religious underpinning for brother-sister marriage, the desire to maintain the "purity" of their Greek origin was the primary reason the Ptolemies followed the tradition. Some have speculated that this inbreeding was the reason for so many weak, unhealthy rulers late in the Ptolemaic dynasty, although Cleopatra was an obvious exception.

Because of the intermarrying, however, Cleopatra was probably mostly of Greek descent. There is some uncertainty about the origin of her paternal grandmother. While she was probably Greek, at least one of the other Ptolemies was known to have taken an Egyptian mistress. There has also been speculation that she was Syrian.

Still, the question of Cleopatra's race had been a matter of considerable debate for decades. Most scholars agree that she was probably Greek, if only because no mention was ever made of her race by her Roman detractors, who by all accounts were extremely sensitive to differences in appearance and background.

As Cleopatra grew older, Egypt was threatened from outside and from within. Many were growing angry about her father's decadence, while personal family feuds weakened the royal family. On the outside, the powerful armies of Rome were methodically expanding its hold around the entire Mediterranean world.

two

THE SHADOW OF ROME

Although Egypt was still officially a sovereign kingdom when Cleopatra was born, in reality it had been an unofficial city state of Rome for more than one hundred years. After defeating Carthage in the Second Punic War, in 202 B.C., Rome had emerged as the most powerful client state in the world. Under a succession of generals, the powerful city state had conquered most of Greece and Macedonia, as well as parts of northern Africa and Asia Minor—modern day Turkey.

Soon after the end of the second war with Carthage, Rome began sending "ambassadors" to Egypt. When Ptolemy V became pharaoh, Rome sent a guardian to protect him, and later intervened to defend Egypt when other countries threatened invasion. Cleopatra's grandfather, Ptolemy VIII Euergetes, who was nicknamed Fatty because of his immense bulk, had to ask for Rome's help putting down an insurrection of his own people. This dangerous habit of appealing to Rome for help continued after Cleopatra was born.

The Romans considered their city to be the center of the world, and in some ways it was. After a territory came under official Roman control a governor was sent out to rule over it. The governors demanded gold, silver, jewels, livestock, and other goods from the subjected people. They also collected taxes from the native peoples, sending a portion of this money back to Rome and hoarding the rest to build up vast treasuries for themselves.

Rome—unlike Egypt—did not have a king or a ruling family. Instead, it was a republic ruled by the Roman Senate. Over the preceding decades the republican form of government had been unable to find a way to successfully incorporate the newly conquered territories into a political system originally designed for a single city state. The armies were usually gone from Rome for years, which meant the powerful generals often led armies more loyal to them

The Roman Senate

personally than to the government back in Rome. Another fear was that the monarchical traditions Romans associated with Egypt and other kingdoms to the East would infect Rome. These concerns caused many prominent Romans to pause before agreeing to an invasion of Egypt, giving the Ptolemies a bit of breathing room.

People who lived within Rome's vast grip were divided into two broad groups—citizens and non-citizens. Citizens had rights and privileges protected under Roman law. In return, they served the republic by voting in elections, fighting in the army, or working in the Roman bureaucracy. The children of Roman citizens were citizens, as were freed slaves and those who had done great service to Rome. Citizens were either patricians or plebeians. The patricians, or landowners, were the leading citizens of Rome and held most of the wealth and power. In the early centuries of the Republic the plebeians were poor and had little or no land of their own. Most worked as manual laborers, although some had jobs as artisans and shopkeepers. As time went on, however, and Rome expanded, some plebeian families became wealthy and began to exercise political power.

The majority of people who lived in Roman territory were not citizens. Those living in Roman controlled areas were not citizens or slaves, who were owned by others, and had no rights. Noncitizens could not vote in elections but had to pay taxes.

The Roman Senate was made up of a group of about three hundred men from either patrician or wealthy plebeian families. Two magistrates, called consuls, were elected by the Senate and alternated monthly as president of the body. Once appointed, consuls, along with all other magistrates, served in the Senate for life and were expected to spend large amounts of money entertaining, providing for their supporters, and paying for public buildings. Although the Senate was not vested with the authority to make laws (that duty was reserved for the popular assemblies), it exercised considerable authority in Roman politics and had the power to appoint governors, declare war, and appropriate public funds.

As the Roman Republic expanded by conquest, military heroes began to dominate Roman politics. In 60 B.C., when Cleopatra was about ten years old, three popular generals, Julius Caesar, Gnaeus Pompey, and Marcus Crassus effectively seized control of the Roman government, although they did so with the Senate's approval. This triumvirate, or group of three, acted as Rome's unofficial heads of

In 60 B.C., Julius Caesar, Marcus Crassus, and Gnaeus Pompey (from left) formed a triumvirate to rule the Roman Republic. (Caesar, courtesy of Réunion des Musées Nationaux/Art Resource; Crassus courtesy of Bridgeman Art Library; Pompey, courtesy of The Granger Collection)

state. All three men were from a patrician faction called the *Populares*, who used the lower assemblies and their own popularity to challenge the power of another patrician faction known as the *Optimates*.

Each triumvir, as each of them were known, dominated one area of Roman politics. Crassus had great influence over the tax collectors in the provinces, who controlled the source of Rome's great wealth. Pompey controlled almost all of the Roman legions stationed in Italy. Caesar, who controlled troops in Gaul, was immensely popular among the plebeians for his generosity with the bounty he brought back and distributed among them, which gave him influence in the popular assemblies. The alliance was not an official

Roman banquet
(Courtesy of The
Granger Collection)

pact, but a mutually convenient arrangement. Rome was still a republic in theory only. There was tension within the triumvirate as each man competed for the people's loyalties with public feasts, games, and lavish displays of wealth.

The spoils of conquest had made Rome wealthy. A favorite activity among the upper class was to eat extravagant foods. These wealthy Romans ate bread with honey for breakfast; eggs, cheese, cold meats, and fruit for lunch; and roast poultry or fish for dinner. Spiced, sweet, diluted wine was consumed at most meals, along with goat's milk. Banquets sometimes lasted as long as ten hours, and often consisted of eggs, sardines, mushrooms, flamingo tongues, elephant trunks, and fattened dormice sprinkled with honey and sesame seeds. These diners tickled their

Seneca (ca. 4 B.C.–A.D. 65), one of Rome's greatest Latin prose writers, lived during the reign of Augustus. (Courtesy of Bildarchiv Preussischer Kulturbesitz/Art Resource)

The Roman forum became the general gathering place of the city. (Courtesy of The Granger Collection)

throats with feathers in order to induce vomiting so they could eat more. "They vomit to eat, and eat to vomit," wrote Seneca, a Roman philosopher.

As Rome spread in all directions, it built new towns and rebuilt old ones in the traditional Roman style. Straight, paved streets organized into methodical grids were lined with different shops, taverns, restaurants, and markets where one could buy anything from sandals to vegetables to slaves. In the middle of the town was the forum, a large market square where people played games, bought and sold items, and paid their taxes.

Rome itself had a population of about one million people, compared to Alexandria's six hundred thousand. Most Romans lived in apartment-type buildings that sometimes were seven floors high. They were forbidden

Roman aqueduct (Courtesy of Vanni/Art Resource)

to light fires inside the apartments because they were built of wooden beams. Instead they bought hot foods like pies, sausages, breads, porridges, and stews from snack bars in the streets. Most Romans did not have running water or toilets and kept buckets and used community pay toilets, which also served as places for social gatherings and discussions. Running water, from a system of pipes and channels called aqueducts, supplied water for public bathhouses, toilets, and drinking fountains.

Wealthier Romans lived in beautifully decorated mansions, called villas. Paintings and statues adorned the interior rooms and colorful mosaics covered the walls and floors. Many of these homes were equipped with underfloor heating, bakeries, pools, and gardens. Wealthy Romans lived, in fact, much like wealthy Alexandrians, although perhaps not quite as magnificently.

ABOVE: *Bust of Aristotle*
(Courtesy of Alinari/Art
Resource)

RIGHT: *Bust of Plato*
(Courtesy of Bildarchiv
Preussischer Kulturbesitz/Art
Resource)

Cleopatra's era was a time of great cultural exchange. Merchant traffic and trade expansion in the Mediterranean region brought a mix of people from the East, Greece, Egypt, and even as far away as Gaul (modern day France) and Britannia (Britain), into the region's thriving urban centers. The Romans admired Greek civilization and culture and emulated Greek architecture, such as bathhouses, theaters, amphitheaters, fountains, and arches. The writings of ancient Greek philosophers such as Plato and Aristotle were also popular among Romans.

As Rome came to dominate an increasingly large portion of the Mediterranean, Cleopatra's father, Auletes, knew that Egypt was vulnerable. The Egyptian army would be easily defeated by the well-trained, disciplined Roman soldiers, and Rome would seize Egypt's wealth, subjugate the Greeks, and levy new taxes on the population. In an attempt to maintain his throne, Auletes made a deal with Rome, the beginning of a long, complicated relationship in which Egypt would unsuccessfully struggle to maintain its independence.

In 59 B.C., when Cleopatra was ten years old, her father, Auletes, paid the newly formed Roman triumvirate a bribe of six thousand talents, which roughly equaled Egypt's entire revenue for one year. In exchange for the money, the triumvirate agreed to support Auletes's claim to the Egyptian throne against the increasingly rebellious Egyptian mobs. Julius Caesar, who was consul at that time, pushed a resolution through the Roman Senate proclaiming Auletes a "friend and ally of the Roman people."

Although paying a foreign government to recognize him as king was humiliating, Auletes knew he could not survive without Rome as an ally. But the acknowledgement came at a great cost. In order to keep his subjects from having to pay the bribe to Rome at one time, Auletes borrowed the money from a Roman moneylender and planned to spread the new taxes over several years in order to eventually repay the loan. The added interest of the loan only added to the burden.

Despite Auletes's best efforts, tensions between Rome and Egypt escalated. Auletes's subjects resented paying tribute to Rome, and fighting frequently erupted in the streets of Alexandria. When a Roman visitor in Alexandria accidentally

Under the Ptolemaic dynasty, Bastet, a female cat goddess, became the deity of perfumes and the moon. (Courtesy of The Granger Collection)

killed a cat, an animal sacred to Egyptians, he was murdered by an angry mob. Widespread ethnic hatred continued to brew. Greeks and Egyptians thought the Romans were only interested in violence and military glory, while Romans viewed Greeks and Egyptians as weak and degenerate.

Although Romans bore the brunt of the anger, Egypt also turned on itself. While their pharaoh continued his drunken carousing within the luxurious palace walls, his subjects suffered and starved under the burden of the new taxes.

Auletes's bribe lost him what little respect his subjects had retained for him and Rome now saw him as its puppet. His money safely in their coffers, the triumvirs continued to eye his kingdom.

One year after Auletes arranged the bribe, a Roman general and senator named Marcus Porcius Cato seized the Egyptian island of Cyprus that was ruled by Auletes's

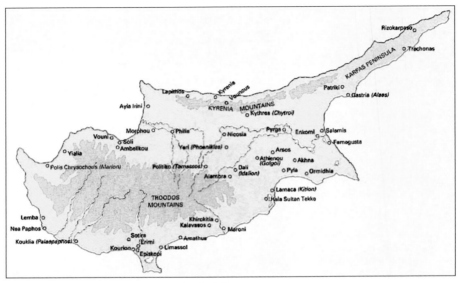

Ancient Cyprus

brother. Rather than face the humiliation of dethronement, Cleopatra's uncle committed suicide. Her father did nothing, which incited riots in the streets of Alexandria. Cleopatra's father fled to Rome, seeking help.

When Auletes abandoned his kingdom, Cleopatra's oldest sister, Cleopatra VI, seized the throne, but was quickly murdered by her sister Berenice, who ruled Egypt with her new husband, a High Priest named Archelaus. With her mother dead and her father far away, Cleopatra had no guide. She warily observed the intrigues and deceptions of the Egyptian court, trying to keep herself alive and steeling herself for the time when she would have to navigate its many perils.

In Rome, Auletes wasted no time in attempting to topple his daughter. When a delegation from Alexandria arrived in Rome to make their case against Auletes to the Romans,

Auletes had most of them murdered and bribe the rest. He then offered an even larger bribe of ten thousand talents to the Roman government in return for their support in attacking Berenice and Archelaus and restoring him to the throne.

Aulus Gabinius, the Roman governor of Syria, sent legions of infantry and cavalry to occupy Alexandria. Terrified, Berenice's soldiers deserted her,

Unidentified Ptolemy queen, usually considered to be Cleopatra. (Courtesy of Alinari/Art Resource)

and she was quickly captured. Her father ordered her execution. After Berenice's death, Roman ships docked in Alexandria's harbors and began transporting chests of grain and money back to Rome to pay Auletes's most recent debt.

Upon his return to Egypt, Cleopatra's father staged a grand celebration. Spectators were given a lavish meal, and watched a parade of thousands of oxen, dogs, elephants, giraffes, Indian parrots, a gnu, and a large white bear. The celebration was just a pretense though. A Roman creditor had been appointed head financial minister, and Auletes

A relief sculpture depicting a sibling marriage in the Egyptian Royal Family
(Courtesy of Giraudon/Art Resource)

levied even heavier taxes on his people to help pay his considerable debt.

An uneasy peace settled over Alexandria for the next few years. Everyone knew the ruler of Egypt was in Rome's pocket and that the Romans could not be kept at bay much longer. In 51 B.C., an aging Auletes began to consider his successor and turned his attention to his intelligent and skillful daughter Cleopatra. As a royal princess, she already held a powerful position in Egypt and had experience dealing with court. Her title, Cleopatra VII Thea

Philopator, meant "Goddess and Lover of her Father and Fatherland."

Unlike women in most other countries in the first century B.C., Egyptian women retained many personal and legal rights. They held jobs and could own property, buy and sell it if they chose, and will it to whomever they wished without anyone's permission. Egyptian women were able to bring a case to the courts if they felt they had been wronged and their judgment and understanding was seen as equal to a man's. Yet, despite their relatively high standing in Egyptian society, royal women were not named sole rulers. They were required to have a king beside them.

Auletes designated his oldest living child, eighteen-year-old Cleopatra, as his heir with the condition that she rule jointly with her younger half-brother, ten-year-old Ptolemy XIII, a child whose experience was limited to the palace in Alexandria, while Cleopatra had spent several years observing her father's struggles.

Cleopatra had many strong female ancestors to serve as role models. Years earlier, both Arsinoë II and Berenice II had helped to shape their husband's reigns. Her ancestor Cleopatra I Syra had served as vizier under her husband, Ptolemy V, and then exercised sole power upon his death in 180 B.C. Cleopatra I had ruled so effectively that after her reign most of Egypt's queens had taken the name Cleopatra in homage.

Cleopatra would rule with her younger brother when Auletes died, and would also have to marry him, following the custom of sibling marriage among Egyptian royalty.

Most women in Egypt married at thirteen or fourteen years and the woman's parents often arranged a marriage. Divorce was possible, but most marriages ended when one partner died, which was usually around the age of forty. Women regularly died in childbirth, while men generally died from accidents or wars. Diseases such as polio and leprosy took their toll on both the young and the old.

The last few months of Cleopatra's father's reign remain shrouded in mystery. From February to July of 51 B.C., Auletes was either dead, and Cleopatra hid the news so she could quietly seize control, or he was ill and incapable of ruling. By the time Auletes' death was announced in May 51 B.C., the situation had shifted in Cleopatra's favor. The young queen began to exclude her weak and inexperienced younger brother. She left his name off of important documents, kept his image off of coinage, and enlisted the support of many of her father's advisers at court.

Despite her growing dominance, Cleopatra went through with the marriage to her brother. The wedding took place in two ceremonies, one Greek, the other Egyptian. Even before becoming queen, Cleopatra had been considered a goddess, and during the Greek ceremony, she dressed as Aphrodite, the Greek goddess of love. For the Egyptian ceremony, she dressed as Isis, wearing a red, white, and yellow robe edged with a woven band of fruits and flowers. Draped over her shoulders was a black cape embroidered with gold stars and a red moon, and the royal crown of Egypt, topped by a cobra, the sacred serpent of the Nile River, sat atop her head. Female servants outlined her eyes with makeup and shadow, softened her skin with lotions, and scented her body with delicate, expensive perfumes imported from Arabia and India.

Subjects awed by Cleopatra's godlike figure believed she had the support of oracles. An oracle was a statement or prophecy made by a god through a priest or priestess, usually at a shrine or temple. Oracles had a powerful influence and were often manipulated by leaders to lend divine legitimacy to their own reigns or policies. "And while Rome will be hesitating over the conquest of Egypt," predicted one oracle, "then the mighty Queen will appear among men."

But just as Cleopatra was beginning to fulfill the oracles' predictions, a devious group of courtiers were scheming against her. Led by an ambitious eunuch (a castrated man) named Pothinus, the conspirators were advisers to Ptolemy XIII who planned to dethrone Cleopatra and make her brother the sole ruler of Egypt. They began by teaching the young king to hate and envy his sister.

three

QUEEN OF EGYPT

Soon after coming to power in 51 B.C., Cleopatra set off on a goodwill tour of Egypt, from its western deserts to the lush banks of the Nile. Cleopatra's home in the northern part of her kingdom was called Lower Egypt, because it was downstream of the Nile. Her trip began in the southern part of her kingdom, a land she had never seen before, that was called Upper Egypt because it was located upstream, closer to the source of the Nile. It experienced harsher weather and poorer living conditions and the two areas had vastly different dialects, customs, and interests.

Traveling and making herself known to her subjects boosted Cleopatra's popularity, especially in Upper Egypt. The people of this area were less urban, and the population

Giza Pyramids, near Cairo, Egypt (Courtesy of the Associated Press)

was made up of fewer Greek settlers and more Egyptian priests. Traditionally, they were resentful of the rulers in Alexandria. These native Egyptians took advantage of the frequent strife and infighting of the Ptolemaic dynasty to stage rebellions. Cleopatra's father had worked hard to repair relations in Upper Egypt. Throughout his reign Auletes sponsored extensive building projects in the area and courted priests and noble families. He showered them with temples and government offices, which they in turn treated as family possessions.

Cleopatra stopped at the town of Thebes, a former royal capital, where local priests asked her to lead a religious ceremony to honor the Egyptian god Amon-Re. As an Egyptian pharaoh, many of Cleopatra's duties were clerical. She helped to perform rituals and ceremonies

An ancient relief sculpture of Amon-Re (Courtesy of The Granger Collection)

believed necessary to ensure the survival of Egypt and the entire world. To please her Greek subjects, Cleopatra also officiated at festivals and sacrifices honoring Greek gods.

The Egyptians were, like the Greeks, polytheistic, meaning they worshiped many different gods. Re was the sun god. Horus was the god of heaven, or the sky. Osiris was the god of the dead and the underworld. His sister and wife Isis was Egypt's divine mother and the protector of the dead. As traditions changed and merged, different gods occupied different spots in the Egyptian pantheon. For example Amon, a creator god popular in Thebes, eventually merged with Re to become Amon-Re, an all-powerful god. Because he possessed great strength, Amon-Re was symbolized by a living bull, which inhabited his own temple at Thebes and was worshiped by Thebans.

Ancient Egyptians held animals in high esteem. They revered mammals such as baboons, dogs, and cats; reptiles such as crocodiles; and birds such as ibises—all were symbols of various gods and goddesses and served as visual, tangible symbols of divine power. Sometimes ancient Egyptians portrayed their gods and goddesses as humans with animal heads. The sky god Horus, for example, was often depicted as a man with a hawk's head.

Some specific animals were thought to be direct representatives of gods and were defined by markings. A bull of Amon-Re had died before Cleopatra's arrival in Thebes and needed to be replaced. There was a long search for his successor. Egyptians scoured the land for a black bull with the rare markings—a white triangle on its forehead, a white crescent shape on its chest, and a black and white tail. Meanwhile, the previous bull, which had been treated like a pharaoh during its life, was mummified. People rejoiced, sang hymns, and played songs on the flute as the powerful animal was buried.

Many Greek and Roman writers mocked Egyptian religious practices, belittling them as beast-worship, but Cleopatra wisely participated in the mummification ceremony. She wished to show respect for ancient Egyptian beliefs.

Egyptian religion, which was already quite fluid, had become even more amorphous after Alexander's

Mystery Religions

The period of time between 323 B.C., the year of Alexander's death, until Rome seized control of Egypt in 31 B.C, is usually referred to as the Hellenistic Period. During this time, the culture and ideas that had been first developed in Athens and other cities of Ancient Greece became the dominant influence in the areas that had been conquered by Alexander. This Greek influence extended into politics, science, literature, philosophy and religion, and continued well into the Roman era. In religion, the Greek influence was most clearly seen in the development of the so-called mystery religions, which often incorporated ideas from Greek philosophers, such as Pythagoras and Plato.

Pythagoras
(Courtesy of SEF/Art Resource)

The name stems from the ancient Greek word *mysteria*, meaning "initiation." During Cleopatra's life, the groups often focused on worshiping a particular god or goddess, with a goal of attaining a particular outcome, or to answer a question—frequently about the nature of the afterlife—that the state-sponsored public religion did not clarify.

Members of mystery religions often took part in arcane initiation rituals that were kept secret from outsiders. People were usually free to join as many cults as they wished; the cults were not mutually exclusive. Many of them were remarkably egalitarian—men, women, even slaves could join and participate.

One of the largest mystery religions was the Eleusinian mysteries that began in the city of Eleusis in Greece. This religion focused on the myth of the goddess of grain Demeter and her trip into Hades to save her daughter, Persephone. It celebrated the annual harvest, and was believed to ensure healthy crops and a good year. The cult of Isis, which Cleopatra participated in, was another popular mystery religion that continued well into the Roman era.

The mystery religions appealed to those who were looking for a more emotional religion than was offered by the conventional religions, and wanted questions answered regarding how best to live one's life in order to attain immortality. Most of them emphasized the personal spirit or soul of the believer and offered a method the faithful could follow in order to attain salvation and afterlife.

invasion and the subsequent mixing of cultures and religions. Similar gods in Greek and Egyptian traditions were associated with one another. Osiris and the Greek god Dionysus were often paired, as were Isis and the Greek goddess Aphrodite. Sarapis was an amalgam of several Greek and Egyptian gods that Ptolemy I Soter invented to bridge religious gaps between Greeks and Egyptians. Greek and Egyptian gods and goddesses were worshiped together,

This likeness of Cleopatra (left) *bears resemblence to the tomb painting of Isis on the right.* (Library of Congress; Tomb of King Ramses III)

with the Greek names often serving as a thin veneer over ancient Egyptian religious customs and beliefs.

Unlike many earlier Ptolemaic monarchs, who largely dismissed such ceremonies, Cleopatra saw the political value in tying herself to religious symbols. She was one of the first Egyptian rulers in a long time to participate in rituals such as the one replacing the bull at Thebes.

Cleopatra also began styling herself after the goddess Isis. For over two thousand years people from many lands had revered Isis and a cult dedicated to her worship had spread to all corners of the Mediterranean world. Unlike many other gods, who were depicted as animals, Isis was given a human form and a beautiful face. A strong and maternal figure, she was said to champion women and children and hold immense power over both heaven and Earth. Cleopatra commissioned statues and had coins cast depicting her as Isis. As the embodiment of the goddess, Cleopatra became more popular. The Egyptians believed Isis caused the Nile to flood each year, making the land fruitful. It was in this capacity that the early part of Cleopatra's reign fell short.

In the spring of 51 B.C. the Nile failed to overflow its banks. Without the floods the soil grew dry and barren over the summer, leading to scanty harvests and famine. As people grew hungry and desperate, many rebelled or hid in the desert to avoid tax collectors.

The famines of Upper Egypt, however dire, were only the beginning of the problems at the beginning of

Cleopatra's reign. After restoring Auletes to his throne, the Roman general Aulus Gabinus had left behind several legions of soldiers in Alexandria. Although they nominally owed allegiance to Cleopatra, in reality they did as they pleased, and aroused fear and distrust among Greeks and Egyptians, who also continued to fear and distrust one another. Threatened from within, Egypt continued to warily eye the Roman menace.

In a goodwill gesture toward Rome, Cleopatra planned to send troops to help the Roman governor of Syria, Marcus Bibulus, in a military campaign against Parthia. At its greatest reaches, the Parthian Empire encompassed a territory spanning modern day Iran, Iraq, Armenia, parts of Turkey, Georgia, Azerbaijan, Turkmenistan, Afghanistan, Tajikistan, and territories in Pakistan, Syria, Lebanon, Israel, and Palestine. Its stronghold was in modern day Iran, and Rome had repeatedly attempted to conquer the kingdom.

Seeing an opportunity to quell unrest at home, Cleopatra offered Gabinus's former troops to Bibulus. But the men, many of whom had taken wives or had settled in Egypt, were reluctant to return to battle under a severe Roman commander. They mutinied and killed Bibulus's two sons, whom he had sent as messengers.

Not wanting to incur the wrath of Rome, she arrested the murderers and sent them to Bibulus in chains. Many Egyptians viewed her actions as pro-Roman. Cleopatra risked revolts from the army and from the many Alexandrians who had also objected to her father's dealings with

Rome. They saw their queen acting just as her father had done before they drove him out of power.

With this one gesture of good faith toward Bibulus, Cleopatra squandered much of the respect she had earned from her army and her subjects in the early days of her reign. She also aroused the hostility of anti-Roman voices at court, particularly that of Pothinus, her brother's scheming Greek advisor.

Pothinus, like many Greeks, was staunchly anti-Roman. He viewed Romans as untrustworthy, lecherous, and quarrelsome, just as many Romans saw Greeks as arrogant, aggressive, and barbaric. Resenting Cleopatra's loyalty to the Romans they despised, Pothinus and his allies rallied around her ten-year-old brother, and stepped up their campaign to oust Cleopatra.

Cleopatra and her advisor Protarchus had their hands full. Patience was stretched thin throughout the realm and starvation brought on by the poor harvests threatened even Alexandria. By October 50 B.C., Cleopatra had lost the upper hand. A papyrus scroll dated October 27 ordering all grain to be brought to Alexandria was issued in both Cleopatra's and Ptolemy's names, unlike previous decrees, which had listed Cleopatra's name alone. Ptolemy's name also came first, showing that Cleopatra had fallen to second-in-command.

In 49 B.C., Cleopatra fled from Alexandria to Syria, which bordered Egypt to the east. Nothing is known about the specific reasons for her departure or the hazards of her journey. She arrived in Syria with a small band of loyal followers and began to organize support against her brother.

Once in Syria, Cleopatra used her knowledge of Hebrew and Arabic to communicate with local leaders. Determined and crafty, she managed to build up a small army, which probably consisted primarily of mercenaries, and turned back toward Alexandria to reclaim her throne. Ptolemy's councilors, meanwhile, took him to Pelusium, a Mediterranean

Ancient Syria

seaport east of the Nile River delta. With his larger army, Ptolemy was able to block the coastal road and thwart Cleopatra's attempt to return to Alexandria. Brother and sister prepared for a civil war.

Sensing that her army was no match for her brother's,

Cleopatra waited to stage her attack. She was beginning to display a sharp wisdom and intelligence. Meanwhile, an even greater power struggle was taking place in Rome. The generals and triumvirates, Julius Caesar and Gnaeus Pompey, were locked in battle for control. The power struggle began when the third member of the Roman triumvirate, Marcus Crassus, died while fighting in Parthia. Their rivalry soon escalated into a full-scale war.

At fifty-two years old, Julius Caesar was an ambitious and brilliant military commander, politician, writer, and orator. He had already made a conquest of Gaul and was greatly admired by Romans for his courage in battle and his generosity to his soldiers.

Pompey, who enjoyed great support in Italy, joined forces with the *Optimates*, a faction of conservative, mostly patrician, republicans opposed to Caesar and his *Populares*. Pompey's son, Gnaeus, traveled to Alexandria to enlist Egyptian help to defeat Caesar. Pothinus, who now held the Egyptian government in his grip, promised Pompey ships, men, and grain. But, despite Egypt's support, Pompey's forces were soon defeated by Caesar, whose legions had been hardened from fighting fierce campaigns in Gaul and Britain.

After losing a major battle at Pharsalus in northern Greece, Pompey fled to Egypt to ask Ptolemy to help finance another campaign against Caesar. He arrived in Pelusium just as Ptolemy's forces were preparing to attack Cleopatra. Pompey anticipated a friendly welcome, but Ptolemy's advisors now saw Pompey as the loser in

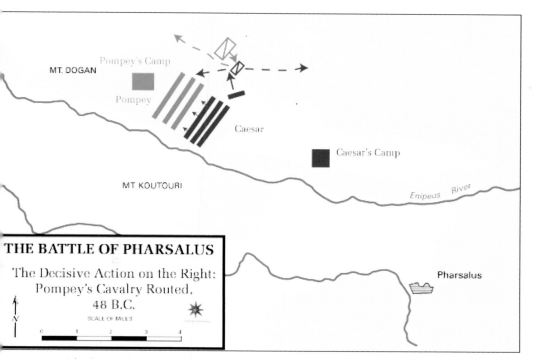

THE BATTLE OF PHARSALUS

The Decisive Action on the Right:
Pompey's Cavalry Routed,
48 B.C.

SCALE OF MILES
0   1   2   3   4

After losing the Battle of Pharsalus, Pompey fled to Egypt to seek aid in his war against Julius Caesar.

the Roman struggle and plotted to murder him in hopes Caesar would be grateful and help them to get rid of Cleopatra for good.

On September 28, 48 B.C., Achillas, an Egyptian general and adviser to Ptolemy, met Pompey's ship in the waters near Pelusium. Achillas told Pompey that the pharaoh's men would row him to shore for a proper welcome. As the soldiers rowed Pompey ashore in a small rowboat, they stabbed him to death and cut off his head, which they planned to present to Caesar as a gruesome token of their friendship. Pompey's crew immediately fled to sea, taking Pompey's wife, Cornelia, to safety with them.

Caesar, meanwhile, was marching toward Egypt in pursuit of Pompey, unaware that his rival was already dead.

He was determined to capture Alexandria, and collect the long overdue debts Cleopatra's father owed Rome in order to pay his soldiers..

Caesar arrived in Egypt with ten ships and four thousand soldiers, and four days after Pompey's death, he arrived in Alexandria. With great ceremony, Ptolemy and his advisers offered him Pompey's severed head, which they had pickled in brine. But to their surprise, Caesar grew visibly upset that Pompey, who had once been his close friend, had been treacherously stabbed in the back. He ordered the execution of Pompey's murderers, and had Pompey's remains returned to his wife Cornelia in Italy, where he was honorably buried.

His present to Caesar a disaster, Ptolemy was in no position to make demands. He and his advisers nervously waited for Caesar to leave, but he remained in Alexandria, occupying the royal palace and collecting on his debts by raiding the Egyptian treasury. Caesar did not want to hurry back to Rome, where Pompey had been popular.

Caesar had played a role in restoring Cleopatra's father to the throne, and now claimed he wanted to honor Auletes's wish of having Cleopatra and her brother rule together. In reality, Caesar wanted to maintain a level of control over Egyptian affairs. If he succeeded in negotiating a compromise, both parties would be indebted to him and to Rome. Caesar also knew that an end to the civil war would make it easier to collect tribute from Egypt. He summoned both Cleopatra and Ptolemy to the royal palace in Alexandria.

Ptolemy and his advisers were not interested in Caesar's plans to end the conflict, however. They were in the superior position, with their hands on the reins of power, and refused to compromise. Instead, they plotted to chase Caesar and his army out of Alexandria. When Caesar requested food supplies for his soldiers, Pothinus had moldy grain delivered to them in order to arouse dissatisfaction and hopefully hasten their return to Rome. Ptolemy and his advisors also stirred up anti-Roman feeling in the streets of Alexandria and street battles broke out.

In the meantime, Ptolemy's army, stationed at Pelusium under Achillas's control, awaited Cleopatra's return. Unlike her shortsighted brother, Cleopatra knew Egypt had no chance against Rome. She was willing to negotiate with Caesar, but Ptolemy's army stood between her and Alexandria. The standing order among Ptolemy's troops was to kill Cleopatra on sight, but she needed to heed Caesar's summons.

According to legend, Cleopatra invented a daring plan to sneak into the royal palace. One night Cleopatra and an ally named Apollodorus slipped into Alexandria's harbor in a small boat. Posing as a merchant, Apollodorus quietly rowed Cleopatra to the palace's private landing where she wrapped herself in a thick, ornate carpet. Apollodorus then slung the carpet, with Cleopatra rolled up inside, over his shoulder and carried the bundle up a marble stairway, into the palace, past the Roman soldiers and Egyptian palace guards, directly into Caesar's chambers. There, as Caesar and his guards watched, Apollodorus unfurled the carpet

Cleopatra emerges from the carpet in which Apollodorus smuggled her into Caesar's presence. (Courtesy of The Granger Collection)

and the queen of Egypt tumbled out before the most powerful man in Rome.

If the legend is true, Cleopatra's dangerous gambit paid off. Ancient historians told tales of Cleopatra enchanting Caesar that evening with her intelligence, charm, wit, and beauty. At only twenty-one, she was probably very alluring to the much older Caesar, who was still said to be lean, tough, and handsome.

Caesar certainly cared about his looks and often tried to conceal his increasing baldness with victory wreaths made of laurel leaves. Attractive to women, he was notorious for his many affairs. At different times, he was known to have had affairs with the wives of both Pompey and Crassus, the other two triumvirs, as well as with the wives of many other prominent Roman politicians. Shrewd and intelligent, he spoke to Cleopatra in Greek and appreciated culture, learning, and the arts.

A romantic rendering of Caesar and Cleopatra. (Courtesy of Réunion des Musées Nationaux /Art Resources)

A detail from the fourth Century B.C. depicting Alexander on horseback
(Courtesy of Erich Lessing/Art Resource)

Undoubtedly, both of these shrewd leaders recognized the political benefits of allying with each other. Caesar was at the peak of his power in Rome, where the senate had made him dictator of the Roman Republic, an absolute, albeit theoretically temporary, position brought on by the civil war. More than anyone else in Egypt, Caesar had the power to restore Cleopatra to her throne. For Caesar, Cleopatra's heritage and wealth could be an asset upon his return to Rome. She was the most recent of a splendid dynasty that was rooted in the conquests of the legendary Alexander the Great, a personal hero of Caesar's, and was the latest in Egypt's three-thousand-year-old line of pharaohs. She was also the queen of the single-wealthiest kingdom in the world.

With physical, mental, and political attraction between them, legend has it that Caesar and Cleopatra became lovers that very night of their first meeting. According to the Roman historian Dio Cassius, Caesar was spellbound by Cleopatra at first glance. As such, most Roman accounts of Cleopatra and Caesar's affair claim that she ensnared and seduced the Roman general as part of a scheme for power. In reality, Caesar had plenty to gain from their affair, and was probably much more sexually experienced.

The morning after Cleopatra's arrival, Caesar invited her thirteen-year-old brother to his quarters. Ptolemy, who did not know that his sister had sneaked into Alexandria, was shocked to find her with Caesar, and was even more dismayed to find that Caesar had taken her side. After their discussion, Ptolemy rushed out into the streets of Alexandria, shouting that someone had betrayed him and his cause was lost. He angrily appealed to the crowd for support against Caesar and Cleopatra. As mobs surged toward the palace, Caesar's men dragged Ptolemy back inside the palace as Caesar ran outside and addressed the crowd, promising to resolve the situation until they dispersed.

Once the riots had subsided, Caesar convened another meeting with Cleopatra and Ptolemy, during which he all but forced the siblings to reconcile. He read Auletes's will aloud and noted that their father had designated the Roman Republic, of which he considered himself to be the instrument, as his executor. It was therefore his responsibility to enforce their father's wishes.

Afterward, Caesar threw a lavish banquet celebrating Cleopatra and Ptolemy's reunion. Cleopatra dressed in silks and wore pearls from the Red Sea, perhaps to impress Caesar, who reputedly loved pearls.

Caesar announced that Rome would return the island of Cyprus, which had recently been annexed by Marcus Cato, to Egypt, and that Ptolemy XIV and Arsinoë, Cleopatra's younger siblings, would rule the island jointly. While this gesture ingratiated Caesar with the Alexandrians, Romans resented losing the new territory.

Cleopatra agreed to rule jointly with her brother, but she undoubtedly knew that Caesar would ultimately support her if a power struggle ever arose again. She watched and waited, aware that her accord with Ptolemy would be short-lived. Pothinus and his fellow schemers had already turned him against her once. She knew that eventually,

Caesar would have to destroy Ptolemy and his advisors. He would have no other option, as Ptolemy was backed by the Alexandrian political leadership and the Egyptian army, both of whom wanted to keep Rome out of Egypt. Cleopatra alone offered cooperation.

Ptolemy had agreed to the co-rulership only as a ploy to buy time. He and his advisers initially planned to wait until Caesar left Alexandria before trying to usurp the throne again, but they soon grew impatient as Caesar's stay in the city wore on. Egged on by his advisors, Ptolemy decided that killing Caesar was the only solution.

Ptolemy and Pothinus began to plot. First, they attempted to have Caesar poisoned at a banquet. When that failed, they spread rumors in hopes of turning public opinion against Caesar and Cleopatra. Pothinus told the Alexandrians that Cleopatra had surrendered her power to Caesar and hinted that Caesar's troops were few in number and anxious to avoid a fight—with one strong attack, Egypt could be free of Rome forever. In mid-November of 48 B.C., Ptolemy's army of twenty thousand, still led by Achillas, turned toward Alexandria. As they marched into the city and surrounded the palace, where Cleopatra, Ptolemy, and Arsinoë, Cleopatra's younger half-sister, were all ensconced, the people of Alexandria began to riot against the Roman guard and soldiers.

Caesar managed to hold one-quarter of the palace and a portion of the harbor, but was trapped. But his army was hardened and well-disciplined, while the Alexandrian force consisted mainly of runaway slaves, pirates, outlaws, and the remnants of the Roman legions left behind by Gabinus. It was still a very dangerous situation. Caesar was outnumbered five to one, and the crafty Egyptians pumped seawater into the pipes leading to the palace, making the water undrinkable. Unable to survive without water, Caesar's men began to dig wells at night. They discovered fresh water near the shore, but it was behind the battle lines. Soon, fighting began in earnest, and Caesar sent messages to Rome for reinforcements. The struggle for Alexandria had begun.

When Ptolemy took up arms against Caesar, Cleopatra divorced her brother as was her right under Egyptian law. Meanwhile, Arsinoë escaped the palace and joined the Alexandrian troops, whose leader, Achillas, she had murdered and replaced with one of her own advisers, a treacherous man named Ganymedes. Convinced Caesar would lose, Arsinoë proclaimed herself the new queen of Egypt.

But soon after Ganymedes helped secure the throne for Arsinoë, he struck a deal with Caesar to exchange her for Ptolemy, who was still Caesar's captive inside the palace. Caesar was all too happy to hand over the young king, who, if he survived the war, would have to be restored to power with his sister, in accordance with Auletes's will. If he died in battle, on the other hand, Cleopatra could rule without him. Ptolemy begged Caesar not to hand him over to his own troops, but Caesar was firm. But when Ptolemy's advisor Pothinus attempted to join the Alexandrians, Caesar had him arrested and executed for treason. Ptolemy no longer had his principal advisor.

Cleopatra watched from the windows and porches of the palace as Caesar immediately outmaneuvered the Egyptians. First, he captured the island of Pharos and set the Egyptian fleet on fire. The flames spread and burned parts of the Library of Alexandria, destroying nearly forty thousand papyrus scrolls. Despite this irreparable damage to the library, the tables had turned to Caesar and Cleopatra's advantage.

On March 27, 47 B.C., Caesar launched another offensive. Although still outnumbered, his experienced troops fought bravely, while many of the Egyptian soldiers deserted or were easily captured by the Romans. The battle raged on for a day. At one point, after the Egyptians had driven Caesar's troops onto a narrow causeway in the harbor, Caesar was forced to take to the water on an overcrowded ship. Seeing that too many men were following his example and that the boat would soon capsize, Caesar jumped into the harbor. In his heavy armor, he swam about two hundred yards to the safety of another ship, losing only his purple cape. Nearly four hundred of his soldiers died in the battle.

Soon after the skirmish in the harbor, the reinforcements Caesar had called for entered Egypt from across the Sinai Peninsula to the east and quickly captured Pelusium. Caesar marched his troops out of Alexandria and joined forces with the newly arrived legions just north of Memphis, near where the modern city of Cairo now stands. From there the Romans marched south to attack Ptolemy, whose men were in a fortified encampment along the Nile. The vastly superior Roman army overran the fortifications, and Cleopatra's brother boarded a small boat on the Nile, which sank under the weight of too many passengers. Ptolemy's heavy gold armor pulled him down, and he drowned. He was found several days later when someone spotted his armor glittering underwater. Ptolemy's followers consoled themselves that dying in the sacred Nile River was considered a glorious death.

By ancient Egyptian custom, the kingdom needed a male pharaoh. At Caesar's direction, Cleopatra married her younger half-brother, Ptolemy XIV, after making sure that her twelve-year-old co-ruler had no scheming advisers. He was too young to effectively share power or to compete with his older half-sister. Caesar trusted the energetic and bright Cleopatra to rule Egypt as his ally. At twenty-two years old, she had the Roman general's full support. Cleopatra was now the indisputable ruler of Egypt.

four

MURDER
IN ROME

After his victory over Ptolemy, Caesar remained in Egypt for almost a year. He wanted to catalog the plunder and learn more about the land he hoped to absorb into Rome. But there was another, more personal reason, for lingering: Cleopatra was pregnant with his child.

In the late spring of 47 B.C., Caesar and Cleopatra traveled up the Nile River together on her royal barge. They wanted to demonstrate Egypt's strong alliance with Rome. The rural people in Upper Egypt were not as offended by Romans as the Greek Alexandrians were. Many even regarded Rome as a stabilizing influence in Egypt. Cleopatra stood proudly at Caesar's side on the ship's deck,

Cleopatra and Caesar on her Nile barge. (Courtesy of North Wind Picture Archives)

proclaiming her role as queen, ruler, and friend and ally of Rome's strongest leader. The trip also helped Cleopatra to renew her ties with her Upper Egyptian subjects.

Well aware of how pageantry could help shape public opinion, Cleopatra ensured that her barge was a spectacle. It was three hundred feet long, and sixty feet tall, made from cypress and cedar, and decorated with marble. It contained a garden, banquet halls, and staterooms, and could by rowed by oars or powered by sails.

Cleopatra wanted her subjects to identify her as Isis and Caesar as the omnipotent god, Amon-Re, who was married to Isis in some versions of the myth. Although Cleopatra was officially married to her younger, half-brother Ptolemy XIV, she hoped that she could convince her subjects to accept Caesar as her divine husband.

Caesar's soldiers gossiped about Caesar's relationship with Cleopatra and news of it soon filtered back to Rome.

The Roman historian Suetonius commented that Caesar and Cleopatra often feasted together throughout the night, and that the pair "would have sailed together in her state barge nearly to Ethiopia had his soldiers consented to follow him." Many of the soldiers, eager to return home after the long campaign, saw Cleopatra as merely another one of Caesar's mistresses. Caesar was already married to a Roman woman named Calpurnia. He had one child from a previous marriage—a daughter named Julia—who had been married to Pompey when Caesar and Pompey were still united in the triumvirate. Julia had died in childbirth and the child had died as well (women and children frequently died during birth in the ancient world). Caesar hoped his child with Cleopatra would be a son.

Through Cleopatra, Caesar met a Greek astronomer working at the Museum of Alexandria named Sosigenes who had devised an ingenious solution to the problem of the Roman calendar, which was based on lunar cycle. Since twelve lunar months do not constitute a solar year, the Romans had previously counted 355 days in a year, and added an extra month, called an intercalary month, every other year. The Roman Senate had to officially declare this additional month, and did not always do so. After a few years, the Roman calendar no longer matched the seasons. By Caesar's time, the calendar was three months ahead.

For over two thousand years the Egyptians had been using a more accurate calendar based on the sun's 365-day cycle, but the seasons still changed, although more slowly, from year to year because one solar year is actually about

365.25 days. Sosigenes suggested switching to a solar calendar of 365 days a year, divided into twelve months, with an extra day in February every fourth year. Caesar adopted this calendar, and it became known as the Julian calendar. It was further modified in 1582 A.D. by Pope Gregory XIII and was renamed the Gregorian calendar.

Caesar could not stay in Egypt indefinitely. Political affairs in Rome demanded his attention. The Egyptian queen and the Roman general were, however, still useful partners and allies. Caesar needed Egypt's vast wealth and resources and Cleopatra needed Rome's protection. When the allies and lovers parted, Caesar left behind three Roman legions—a total of about twenty thousand men.

After Caesar's departure, Cleopatra threw herself into her administrative duties and set about strengthening her relationship with her subjects. Her work was interrupted during the first week of September 47 B.C., shortly after Caesar left for Rome, when she gave birth to a son she named Caesarion, "Little Caesar." Egyptians interpreted the birth as good luck because he was born on the day of the feast celebrating the goddess Isis. Cleopatra hoped Caesarion would one day rule over a combined Egyptian and Roman empire, with Alexandria as the capital. She had coins minted which show her breast-feeding Caesarion, just as Isis was often depicted feeding her own son, Horus. Sculptors carved the same scene on temples.

En route to Rome, Caesar had to deal with several rebellions that had broken out in northern Asia Minor. He crushed the revolts so quickly that he wrote to a friend,

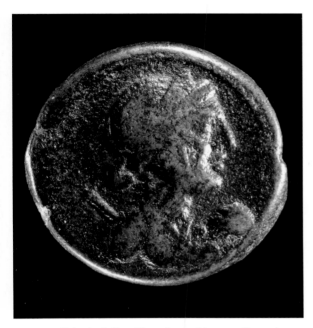

Coin depicting Cleopatra and her son Caesarion.
(Courtesy of HIP/Art Resource)

"Veni, vidi, vici," or "I came, I saw, I conquered."

While he had been gone, Caesar's friend and fellow general Marcus Antonius, or Mark Antony, had watched things for him in Rome, but Caesar returned to unrest. Pompey was dead, but his sons and friends had gathered forces in North Africa to continue the war against Caesar. Although the powerful *Optimates* still opposed him, Caesar pressured the Roman Senate to once again name him dictator. He promised that when the civil war ended, he would relinquish this title. Until then he was to wield absolute power over the entire Roman government and population.

Just as he had in Asia Minor, Caesar quickly put down the revolts in North Africa. Then, shrewdly, he pardoned Pompey's men who had fought against him and restored all of the statues of Pompey, which had been removed from their pedestals. The magnanimous gesture bolstered Caesar's already enormous popularity among common Romans, which awakened further fears among the *Optimates,* who

Mark Antony (Courtesy of Alinari/Art Resource)

were convinced he was on his way to becoming dictator for life. One former senator named Cato, who had sided with Pompey and fled to North Africa, committed suicide rather than live under Caesar.

The Roman Republic had deteriorated from the ideals of democracy it had been founded upon. Many of the senators were viewed as dishonest and inefficient, and had grown corrupt off of the spoils of war. "Those fools think more of saving their fishponds than the republic," said Marcus Tullius Cicero, a great Roman orator, senator, and former consul, about the senate. Cicero penned at least nine hundred letters to his friends and fellow politicians. He wrote about everyday things like the price of bread and bits of scandal, but also wrote about larger issues like wars and political philosophy. After Cato's suicide, Cicero wrote a pamphlet eulogizing him called *Cato*. Caesar, who had shared a long rivalry with Cato, responded with a pamphlet entitled *Anti-Cato*.

Cato (Courtesy of Erich Lessing/Art Resource)

Caesar celebrated his latest military victories with a series of four extravagant victory parades, which the Romans called "triumphs." The festivities commemorated his military successes in Gaul, Egypt, Asia Minor, and North Africa. Caesar wanted the parades to be the richest Rome had ever seen. Lavish floats representing his various victories thronged the Roman Forum. One float showed the Pharos lighthouse in Alexandria with fake flames shooting out of the top of it and another displayed the treasures Caesar had taken during his wars: gold, silver, jewels, and works of art.

Three segments of Andrea Andreani's nine-part painting, The Triumph of Julius Caesar (Library of Congress)

Romans lined the streets to gape in awe. At the end of the procession they saw Caesar with his most important prisoners shuffling behind him in chains, including Cleopatra's sister, Arsinoë. By custom, the prisoners were to be executed by strangulation after the parade, but the sight of the humiliated young Egyptian princess angered many Romans, thus convincing Caesar to spare the girl's life.

Each day, the triumphs ended with an appearance by Caesar, dressed in a purple toga embroidered with gold stars (his dress, modeled after what was worn by pre-Republic kings, symbolized absolute power). Caesar rode in a golden chariot pulled by horses, while his soldiers sang songs praising him.

After the triumphs, Caesar distributed looted treasure to his soldiers and gave one hundred Roman denarii—almost a half a year's pay for an average worker—to every citizen. He also held a feast for Rome's citizens. Romans generally reclined as they ate so Caesar provided 22,000 couches with room on each couch for three diners. There was free food, wine, and entertainment and the feast was followed by a week of games, which people watched

Terra-cotta bas-relief from Campana Collection depicting a deadly contest between lin, lioness, and gladiator (Courtesy of Erich Lessing/Art Resource)

under the shade of silken awnings, an eastern luxury. Hunters shot arrows and threw spears at elephants, lions, and giraffes brought to Rome from northern Africa. Most popular were gladiatorial contests, in which prisoners of war and condemned criminals were forced to fight each other to the death.

In the fall of 46 B.C., Cleopatra received a summons to join Caesar in Rome. She would be recognized as an independent queen and ally of Rome. She sailed to Rome with her son Caesarion, whom Caesar had not yet seen, leaving Egypt in the hands of her loyal advisers and officials. She also brought along her half-brother, Ptolemy XIV, to keep him from scheming against her while she was away. She

Julius Caesar and his wife Calpurnia (Courtesy of Cameraphoto/Art Resource)

traveled with a huge retinue of eunuchs, courtiers, servants, musicians, and scholars, including the astronomer Sosigenes. Upon arrival, they all moved into Caesar's villa on the west bank of the Tiber River, which flows through the center of Rome. Caesar kept a separate villa in another part of the city for his wife, Calpurnia.

Cleopatra's visit caused a sensation in Rome. She was a foreign queen and Caesar's mistress. The concept of a woman with such power was offensive to the conservative *Optimates*, who detested the idea of absolute monarchy, especially one in which the seat of power could belong to a woman.

Caesar made no secret of his relationship with Cleopatra. His marriage to Calpurnia had been a political match, like most marriages among Roman political families. He flaunted their relationship, also frequently showing off Caesarion, the son of their unwed union.

To add to the scandal, Caesar built a new temple honoring Cleopatra. Although it was officially dedicated to the Roman goddess Venus, he had a golden statue depicting Cleopatra as Isis built inside it. Many wondered if Caesar meant to imply that Cleopatra, as Egypt's Isis, was equal to Rome's Venus.

Although Egyptian shrines commonly housed statues of kings and queens portrayed as gods and goddesses, Cleopatra's statue was the first of its kind in Rome. This made it clear that Caesar held Cleopatra in higher regard than any other monarch dependent on Rome, and that their relationship was no casual affair. Some Romans began to suspect that she was manipulating Caesar for her own ends, and that he had already fallen under her influence.

While Cleopatra did have Egypt's interests at heart, she also prompted Caesar to improve Rome. Caesar had clearly been impressed by what he had seen in Cleopatra's realm. Sosigenes, the Egyptian astronomer, helped Caesar to reform the Roman calendar. He had been impressed by the sophisticated waterways built along the Nile and made plans to build canals and drain marshes around Rome to form new waterways like those he had seen in Egypt.

As Caesar began these ambitious projects, Pompey's two sons, who had escaped to Spain, again took up arms. Caesar was forced to go to Spain to put down the revolt, which he did with characteristic speed and efficiency. Upon his return to Rome in February 44 B.C., the Senate appointed him dictator for life. The *Optimates* were convinced Caesar wanted to return to a hereditary monarchy, but the common

Caesar refused the Roman crown when Antony offered it to him. (Courtesy of The Granger Collection)

citizens and soldiers remained loyal to him. He began minting coins with himself depicted in the imperial manner and proclaimed "Men ought to look upon what I say as *law.*"

Yet Caesar hesitated to crown himself king. The Roman people were not ready. He even arranged for Antony to offer him the crown during a Roman fertility festival called the Lupercalia, but Caesar was too savvy to take it, even before the crowd booed. It was all a staged demonstration to convince the citizens he had no intention of becoming emperor. His victories in Africa and Spain had helped him to become dictator, but he would need another dramatic and important conquest to make the people accept him as a monarch.

Early in 44 B.C., Caesar began to plan a campaign to conquer the Parthian Empire, which controlled vast wealth and resources, and, more importantly, was the gateway to fabled India. Caesar, who saw himself as the successor to Alexander the Great, probably intended to extend Rome's grasp well into the Indian subcontinent.

The Parthians had fended off a Roman invasion nine years earlier, killing the triumvir Marcus Crassus and igniting the civil war between Caesar and Pompey. The Romans were eager for revenge. Cleopatra, for her part, probably urged Caesar to claim the throne, divorce Calpurnia, declare Caesarion as his heir, and marry her before leaving for his campaign. Caesar knew, though, that all of these things would be more acceptable to the Romans after he conquered Parthia.

But Caesar had underestimated the resentment mounting against him among the defenders of the

Marcus Brutus (Courtesy of Scala/Art Resource)

Republic. Several prominent Roman senators, led by Marcus Brutus and Longinus Cassius, began meeting to devise a plan to assassinate Caesar. Many of these men, including both Brutus and Cassius, had sided with Pompey during the Civil War and had been pardoned by Caesar in its aftermath. Most had known Caesar their entire life. It was even rumored that Brutus may have been Caesar's son because Caesar had a long affair with his mother, Servilia. Brutus and Cassius's conspirators called themselves the *Liberatores* (liberators) because they believed they were going to free Rome from Caesar's intended tyranny.

"Tyranny must end, Caesar must die," the conspirators whispered among themselves. As rumors of a plot filled Rome, people began to see ominous signs of Caesar's imminent death. They spotted sudden lights in the heavens and heard loud birds disrupting the Forum with their cries. Gruesome stories circulated about sacrificial animals without hearts and one soothsayer, who may have known about the plot, warned Caesar to beware of the Ides, or fifteenth, of March. Caesar ignored the rumors and continued to prepare for his trip to Parthia.

But Caesar's victories were over. On March 14, Caesar and his friend Marcus Lepidus were conversing over some documents Lepidus had brought Caesar to sign. In the course of the conversation, Lepidus asked Caesar what kind of death he thought was best. "A sudden end," Caesar answered. He was about to get his wish.

The next day, as Caesar walked up the steps to enter the Theater of Pompey where the senators were gathering,

Aretemidus, a Greek scholar, handed him a roll of papyrus and indicated that Caesar should read it immediately. The roll contained the details of the conspiracy and the names of the conspirators, but he did not read it.

When Caesar entered the Forum, the conspirators, all of whom were hiding daggers under their cloaks, escorted him to a nearby portico and asked him to read a petition aloud. As he began to read, a senator named Casca produced his dagger, pulled Caesar's tunic aside, and struck him on the shoulder. Caesar wheeled around and grappled with Casca, who called out for help. The other senators pounced, stabbing Caesar twenty-three times while he desperately tried to fight them off.

Caesar at one point fought his way through the throng to the foot of a nearby statue of his former enemy, Pompey. As the blood streamed down his body, Caesar saw

Vincenzo Camuccini's Assassination of Julius Caesar (Courtesy of Scala/Art Resource)

that Brutus was among the conspirators. According to the Roman historian Suetonius, Caesar turned to Brutus and said, "You too, my son?" and then collapsed in a pool of his own blood. Within minutes he was dead. In all, sixty men had taken part in the assassination.

As news of Caesar's murder spread through the streets of Rome, the assassins soon realized few saw them as liberators. Most Romans had viewed Caesar as a hero, and now he was a martyr. Angry mobs roamed the streets and began hunting down and murdering the conspirators; Brutus and Cassius fled to Greece.

At Caesar's villa on the Tiber, Cleopatra received the news from a messenger. She had lost her lover and protector, and her hopes for a unified Egyptian-Roman empire were dashed.

Without Caesar's influence, angry Romans began to speak out against Cleopatra's presence. Cicero wrote, "I hate the queen . . . And the queen's insolence, when she living in Caesar's house in the gardens beyond the Tiber, I cannot recall without indignation."

Cleopatra's prospects looked even more dismal after the reading of Caesar's will. His three great-nephews inherited almost everything. Octavius, the oldest at nineteen, received the largest portion of Caesar's wealth and Caesar had named him his adopted son and heir. Caesar's villa and gardens on the Tiber were bequeathed to the Roman people. He also willed each Roman citizen three hundred sesterces. No mention was made of either Caesarion or Cleopatra because, by law, a foreigner could not inherit Roman property. A rumor spread that Caesar had made

Modern picture of St. Peter's Basilica overlooking the Tiber River. (Courtesy of the Associated Press)

a second will naming Caesarion his heir and that he had been planning to unveil it after he was made king. But as it was, Cleopatra and her son received nothing.

When Octavius, Caesar's adopted son, returned to Rome to claim his inheritance he posed an immediate threat to Cleopatra and her son. Cleopatra thought that Caesarion had a superior claim by virtue of blood and divinity, but she was a realist. With her patron dead, Cleopatra knew that she could easily lose her power—or even her life—if she were captured.

To many Romans, the appearance of a comet confirmed that Caesar's soul had joined the immortal gods in the heavens, but Cleopatra was alone and threatened in Rome. Weeks after Caesar's death, she fled to Ostia, a port at the mouth of the Tiber River, and then home to Egypt. The momentous events of the Ides of March had changed everything.

five

THE QUEEN AND THE GENERAL

Soon after Cleopatra returned to Alexandria, in the summer of 33 B.C., her brother and husband Ptolemy XIV mysteriously died. Some historians speculate that Cleopatra poisoned her fifteen-year-old co-ruler. She certainly stood to benefit from his death because it left her son Caesarion as the only male heir to the throne, but there is no concrete evidence that she was responsible.

Cleopatra proclaimed Caesarion as Ptolemy XV Caesar, her new co-ruler and titled him *Theos Philopator Philometor* or "God who Loves his Father and Mother." His

A relief of the goddess Hathor, preceded by Ptolemy XVI, Caesarion, son of Cleopatra and Julius Caesar, found on the surrounding wall on the Hathor Temple, Dendera, Egypt. (Courtesy of Erich Lessing /Art Resource)

name was intended to remind people that he was Caesar's son. Cleopatra's artists depicted Caesarion on temples as the god Horus, the son of Isis and Osiris. According to Cleopatra, Caesarion was Caesar's heir as his sole surviving child and she hoped that placing her half-Roman son at her side would strengthen her ties to Rome.

Caesar's friend and second-in-command, Mark Antony, gave a moving speech at his funeral. When Antony held up Caesar's bloody toga, the vast crowd of mourners exploded in a frenzy of outrage and grief. Octavius, who presided over the ceremony, titled himself Caius Julius Caesar Octavian,

In this painting Octavian is observing Caesar's wounds, while Antony gives his famous oration against the assassins. (Courtesy of Bridgeman Art Library)

and *Filius Divi Julii,* meaning "Son of the divine Julius," to attract Caesar's soldiers and supporters to him. The wily Octavius knew that, although Caesar had named him his heir, he would soon be locked in a struggle with Antony, who had been at Caesar's side for years.

Cleopatra, and most Romans, sided with Antony. Few knew Octavian well because he had spent most of his early career outside of Rome. Antony was well-respected and adored by soldiers and citizens alike. Antony, as well as Cleopatra, scoffed at Octavian's new title and called him the man "who owes everything to a name." But Antony was underestimating Octavian, who was more intelligent, ambitious, and calculating than anyone had suspected. Octavian quickly mastered the treacherous politics of Rome

Cicero (Courtesy of Alinari/Art Resource)

with the aid of powerful advisors. Cicero, for example, advised him on how to handle the public: "Give them games, bread, wine, spare them from war and improve their lives. This is all they ask."

After a brief, tense period when it looked as though another Roman civil war was inevitable, Antony and Octavian agreed to work together to pursue and punish the conspirators who had murdered Caesar. Antony, Octavian, and Marcus Lepidus, the patrician politician who had spoken to Caesar on the eve of his assassination, formed a second triumvirate. They compiled long lists of their enemies and accused several thousand people of taking part in the conspiracy against Caesar. Hundreds were ruthlessly murdered and their land and money seized. Over the objections of Octavian, Cicero, who had frequently spoken out against Antony, was one of the men killed. According to legend, Antony's third wife, Fulvia, stuck a golden hair pin through the tongue of Cicero's severed head, indicating an end to Cicero's speechs.

Over the next three years, Cleopatra ruled Egypt undisturbed by a preoccupied Rome. As it had during the beginning of her reign, the Nile failed to flood for two years in a row, causing disastrous famines. Egyptians grew so desperate that some began to sell themselves into slavery for food.

Unlike during the previous famine, this time Cleopatra was unfettered by intrigues at court and moved quickly to alleviate the situation. She opened up the extra granaries in Alexandria to distribute grain and prohibited tax gatherers, notorious for gouging the poor, from taking advantage of the situation.

The peace Cleopatra established allowed Alexandrian merchants to improve their trading and business and finally relieved of Auletes's burdensome debts to Rome, the Egyptian economy revived. Her father had nearly ruined Egypt, and now Cleopatra carefully controlled the realm's finances.

Cleopatra took care to remain popular with her subjects, although she had seen with Caesar that popularity alone could not protect a ruler. In addition to the popularity she gained by lowering taxes, she also observed the traditional religious rites and continued to depict herself as the New Isis. She gave food and money to religious temples and curried favor with the priesthood. She was the first Ptolemaic ruler to speak and write in the Egyptian language.

Even Greek Alexandrians, who had resented Cleopatra's ties to Rome, admired her diplomatic skill and commitment to Egyptian independence. She also wanted to regain Egypt's lost colonial possessions of Syria, Judaea, Palestine, and Lebanon, but knew that she needed another strong military leader, like Caesar, to protect her from Roman annexation first. For the moment, she bided her time.

Confusing reports came from Rome where alliances shifted rapidly. When Antony and Octavian raised an army to fight Brutus and Cassius in Greece, Cleopatra realized another Roman civil war was imminent and built a fleet of ships. She knew that the both sides of the feuding Romans would need ships and wanted to be in a strong bargaining position.

Cleopatra decided to throw her support behind the triumvirate. Though she was wary of Octavian,

A drawing of Brutus and Cassius based on Shakespeare's Julius Caesar. (Courtesy of The Granger Collection)

who seemed poised to take much of what Cleopatra considered to be Caesarion's birth right, she was not ready to trust Brutus and Cassius, the men who had murdered her former lover and the father of her son. This also gave her an opportunity to solve another nagging problem. After Caesar's death, Egyptians thought of Cleopatra as a widow. But the Roman troops he had left to protect her clashed with the local population and placed a burden on the economy. She shrewdly turned the legions over to Caesar's loyal friend Publius Dolabella, who was fighting his own campaign against Caesar's murderers in Greece. As the Roman troops departed, they painted graffiti on buildings throughout Upper Egypt, including the royal tombs in Thebes and the walls of the temple of Isis at Philae along the Nile in southeastern Egypt.

In exchange for the four legions, Caesar's supporters, led by Antony and Octavian, agreed to recognize Caesarion as Caesar's son and Cleopatra's co-ruler, even though Octavian knew that Caesarion weakened his own claim.

Cleopatra kept the pact with the triumvirate a secret from Brutus and Cassius, who continued to ask for her support. Cassius even managed to persuade Serapion, Cleopatra's viceroy in Cyprus, to give him several Egyptian ships without the queen's consent. But when the former conspirators pressed Cleopatra for further assistance, she put them off, telling Cassius that because of the recent famine she could not send ships or aid. Meanwhile, she prepared ships and troops to join the forces of the triumvirate.

When Brutus and Cassius discovered her duplicity, they decided to invade Egypt. Cleopatra set out to sea to meet their attack, commanding her own fleet of warships. She was the first woman to command a navy in battle since Artemesia, a Greek warrior queen, centuries earlier. She sailed northwest to meet Antony and Octavian, who had just left Italy. A few days out of the harbor, however, her fleet ran into a violent storm. Several ships sank, and Cleopatra fell ill, and they were forced to return to Alexandria.

Regardless, Cassius and Brutus's invasion of Egypt was not to be. In October 42 B.C., Antony and Octavian defeated them at the Battle of Philippi in northern Greece. Both Brutus and Cassius committed suicide in the wake of their loss. The new triumvirate now ruled Rome almost absolutely, although all three claimed to want nothing more than to restore the republic—at some point, when it was safe.

The three men split up the provinces with Antony taking the lion's share. Having led Roman troops at the Battle of Philippi—Octavian had taken a minor role and Lepidus had stayed behind in Italy—Antony was the most powerful triumvir. He took control of Gaul and the wealthy eastern provinces, including Asia Minor, Syria, and Greece. Octavian took Spain and the western Mediterranean, including Sardinia. Lepidus, the least powerful triumvir, ruled North Africa. Italy was to be ruled jointly by all three, but Octavian quickly gained control there.

Antony, at forty-five years old, had emerged from the chaos as a formidable leader. He was already well-known for his military prowess, but after Caesar's murder he had revealed that he could be a shrewd politician, capable of containing and exploiting a volatile situation. Strong and handsome, Antony resembled statues of the ancient hero Hercules with his muscular build and curly hair. He even claimed to be descended from Hercules, belting his toga low over his hips and swaggering like the hero. Unlike the more sophisticated Caesar, Antony pursued physical rather than intellectual recreations. He dined with his soldiers, ate heavily, drank, and danced. He also enjoyed the company of musicians, dancers, and actors.

As Antony's armies journeyed east to occupy his new territories, he staged many grand celebrations along the way, paid for by heavy taxes on Rome's eastern provinces. Antony celebrated in style and taxed so excessively that one of his tax collectors quipped to him: "If you intend to raise two taxes a year, you must also see to

Statue of Hercules and Cacus (Courtesy of Timothy McCarthy/Art Resource)

it that each year contains two summers and two autumns for harvesting."

Despite the heavy taxes, Antony was hailed as the "emperor of the east" as his armies marched through Greece and Asia Minor. Some even began to worship Antony as the New Dionysus and carved statues of him in that guise. Dionysus, like Isis, was a savior god worshipped in cults throughout the eastern Mediterranean. He was also the god of wine and revels, an identity that suited Antony's outgoing, gregarious personality.

Antony hoped to take up Caesar's quest to conquer Parthia, which would prove that he, and not Octavian, was the worthy successor of Caesar. But if Parthia was to be the path to Antony's imperial ambitions he would need money. For this he turned to Cleopatra.

Artist's rendition of Cleopatra's ship landing at Tarsus, where she met Mark Antony. (Courtesy of Giraudon/Art Resource)

Antony summoned the Egyptian queen to the town of Tarsus on the coast of what is now southern Turkey. Situated at the foot of Mount Tarsus, the town had a flourishing port and a renowned school of rhetoric at which both Caesar and Cato had studied. Cleopatra did not answer Antony's first summons and also ignored his second. It would not do to come running when he beckoned. Finally, at his third command, she set sail for Tarsus. Egypt's fate depended on Antony, but Cleopatra was determined to establish that she was the queen of an independent kingdom, not a Roman subordinate who could be ordered around at will. It was bold of Cleopatra to keep Antony waiting, but she had seen her father go begging to Rome with disastrous consequences. Even after departing, she took her time arriving in Tarsus, keeping Antony on tenterhooks.

Cleopatra arrived at Tarsus by sailing up the river Cydnus in her lavish barge, showing herself to be a proud, independent, and majestic ruler. When people saw the Egyptian queen, they flocked to her, swarming to the river's banks to gaze in wonder. It was said that the delicate scent of her perfume wafted to shore as she reclined under a gold cloth canopy as young boys cooled her with large fans. Plutarch wrote:

> She came sailing up the river Cydnus in a barge with gilded stern and outspread sails of purple, while oars of silver beat time to the music of flutes and fifes and harps. . . . Her maids were dressed like sea nymphs and graces, some steering the rudder and others working at the ropes.

Cleopatra dressed for her audience with Antony as Aphrodite, the Greek goddess of love. At first Antony stayed ashore with a small entourage, waiting for her to come to him before sending her an invitation to meet over a banquet. When Cleopatra invited him to the waterside to meet her, Antony gracefully accepted and climbed aboard her barge. "He found the preparations to receive him magnificent beyond expression," wrote Plutarch. "The whole thing was a spectacle that has seldom been equaled for beauty."

Antony was clearly dazzled. They dined on grapes, figs, dates, wild hare, gazelle, purple shellfish, peacocks, cranes,

The meeting of Antony and Cleopatra as depicted by Sir Lawrence Alma-Tadema.
(Courtesy of Bridgeman Art Library)

Some of Antony's followers began worshipping him as the new Dionysus, the Greek god of wine, agriculture, and theater. In Caravaggio's painting, Dionysus goes by his Roman name, Bacchus. (Courtesy of The Granger Collection)

oysters, berries, nuts, wines, cheeses, and breads, while small lanterns hung from tree branches overhead. Throughout the meal, actors, acrobats, clowns, dwarfs, gladiators, dancers, and musicians entertained Cleopatra and her guest.

The following evening Antony invited Cleopatra to dine at his quarters in Tarsus. Antony's banquet was a much more rustic affair, but Cleopatra quickly adapted, exchanging coarse repartee with her host and his soldiers. "Perceiving that his raillery was broad and gross, and that it savored more of the soldier than of the courtier, she rejoined in the same taste, and fell at once into that manner, without any sort of reluctance or reserve," wrote Plutarch.

There was a strong attraction between them. Cleopatra was drawn in by his strength, and Antony was intrigued by her lavish lifestyle. Plutarch wrote of her:

> Her actual beauty . . . was not in itself so remarkable that none could be compared with her. . . . But the

contact of her presence, if you lived with her, was irresistible; the attraction of her person, joining with the charm of her conversation, and the character that attended all she said or did, was something bewitching. It was a pleasure merely to hear the sound of her voice, with which, like an instrument of many strings, she could pass from one language to another.

Antony might also gain politically from a relationship with the queen. Although he currently held the upper hand over Octavian, Antony was not related to Caesar. If Antony took up Caesarion's cause and defeated Octavian, he could rule Rome as Caesarion's regent. He and Cleopatra soon became lovers.

Despite their affair, Antony and Cleopatra were still political leaders who needed to conduct business with one another. She agreed to supply money and soldiers for Antony's Parthian campaign. In exchange, he promised to order the deaths of Serapion, the viceroy of Cyprus who had given troops to Cassius, and of Arsinoë, Cleopatra's only living sibling, whose life Caesar had spared during his triumph through Rome and now lived in Ephesus, where she plotted to overthrow Cleopatra. With Arsinoë's death, Cleopatra would have no more threatening siblings.

Antony traveled to Alexandria to spend the winter of 41–40 B.C. as Cleopatra's guest. He came as a private citizen, without his soldiers, so Alexandrians would not fear a Roman occupation. He wanted to bide his time in Egypt in the hopes that tensions would ease in Rome in his absence, but at least part of the reason for his stay was pleasure. Cleopatra and Antony held extravagant parties, which often spilled out into the streets of Alexandria. Antony loved feasting, dancing, gambling, and bawdy jokes. They surrounded themselves with young, wealthy Alexandrians and titled themselves "The Inimitable Livers."

At night they would go into the streets of Alexandria disguised as commoners, in search of fun. They would drink among peasants, or knock loudly on doors and run away before the residents could open them. Occasionally they were caught by servants and, according to Plutarch, "were very scurvily answered and sometimes even beaten severely, though most people guessed who they were."

Exaggerated tales of their drunken escapades became gossip in Rome. Cleopatra's enemies said she was constantly drunk and only managed to appear sober because she wore a magical trinket. Others claimed that she was recklessly trying to impress Antony with her wealth. According to one story, she bathed in donkey's milk to soften her skin. In another story, Cleopatra bet Antony she could spend ten million sesterces on a single banquet. When she served him an ordinary meal, he teased her. But for the second course, she removed an expensive pearl earring, dissolved it in a cup of vinegar, and swallowed the solution, winning the bet. The story is highly suspect, since vinegar cannot dissolve pearls and any acid strong enough to do so would almost certainly have killed her. Regardless, the story fascinated and horrified Romans who viewed pearls as symbols of opulence.

Cleopatra planned elaborate hunting and fishing trips. On one trip, when an embarrassed Antony was not catching any fish, he secretly hired some fishermen to swim underwater and attach previously caught fish to his hook. When he began pulling in fish, Cleopatra discovered his trick. The next day when they went fishing again, she sent down a diver with an old, dry, salted fish to attach to his fishhook. Everyone laughed when Antony pulled out the long-dead fish. "Emperor, you had better give up your rod. . . . Your sport is to hunt cities and kingdoms and continents," Cleopatra chided Antony.

Antony planned to leave Egypt in the spring and resume planning his campaign against Parthia, but disturbing news forced him to leave earlier. Several neighboring territories had joined Parthia and attacked Syria. Most of Antony's troops were in Greece, Gaul, and Italy. In addition, Antony's wife, Fulvia, and his brother, Lucius, had led an unsuccessful uprising against Octavian in Italy. Fulvia fled to Greece and died soon afterwards. Lucius was captured, but Octavian forgave him and made him governor of Spain.

Antony had no choice but to leave. Once again, Cleopatra was abandoned by her Roman consort, and once again she was pregnant with a Roman general's child.

six

ON HER OWN

Not long after Antony left for Italy in the fall of 40 B.C, Cleopatra gave birth to twins, a boy and a girl. She named her new son Alexander Helios, after the legendary Alexander the Great and the Greek sun-god, Helios. Her daughter was named Cleopatra Selene, after herself and the Greek moon-goddess, Selene.

Cleopatra now ruled alone and unopposed. All of her siblings were dead and the army was loyal to her. Because Antony supported her, no foreigner would dare attack Egypt. But she remained cautious, even sending her astrologer back to Italy with Antony to relay news back to her and to remind Antony not to trust Octavian.

Cleopatra would not see Antony again for the next three and a half years. Antony focused on making peace with Octavian, and distancing himself from his late wife's

Cleopatra's son Alexander Helios was named after Alexander the Great and the Greek sun-god, Helios, shown here on an ancient vase.

failed revolt. He arranged for a meeting with Octavian to be held at the seaport of Brundisium, in southeastern Italy on the Adriatic Sea, but Octavian stood him up. Octavian had not honored another agreement to share Italy equally when it came time to recruit and quarter soldiers. Octavian had seized more than his share of land and was siphoning men from Antony's legions.

In October of 40 B.C., the two men finally met. Despite the tensions, they made peace, primarily because few Roman soldiers wanted to fight another Roman civil war. In the Treaty of Brundisium, Antony ceded Gaul to Octavian but kept his eastern territories. They renewed the triumvirate, although they increasingly ignored their third partner, Lepidus. Antony and Octavian sealed the pact with a marriage between Antony and

This coin, minted in celebration of the reconciliation between Antony and Octavian, shows Antony's new wife, Octavia. (Courtesy of Bildarchiv Preussischer Kulturbesitz/Art Resource)

Octavian's sister, Octavia. Romans, hopeful for a new era of peace, rejoiced.

Word of Antony's marriage to Octavia reached Cleopatra two weeks after she gave birth to their twins. The news was a blow to her pride and ambitions. Octavia was young, demure, and popular among the Romans, many of whom still remembered Cleopatra as willful and frivolous. But Cleopatra had one advantage: although Octavia soon gave birth to a baby daughter, Cleopatra had provided Antony with a male heir. Nevertheless, Antony was living in Rome with his new wife and their child, while Cleopatra remained in Alexandria.

Over the next few years, Cleopatra was busy both as a queen and a mother. During this time, several books were published under her name. She might have written them or had them commissioned to be issued under her name. One was on weights, measures, and coins, another

The favorite wife of Ramses II, Nefertari, demonstrates the Egyptian standard of beauty in the paintings that adorn her tomb.

on medicine and gynecology, a third on alchemy, and a fourth on cosmetics. The cosmetics book contained this cure for baldness:

> Of domestic mice, burnt, one part; . . . of horse's teeth, burnt, one part; of bear's grease, one part; of deer marrow, one part; of reed-bark, one part. To be pounded when dry and mixed with lots of honey; and the bald part rubbed (with this mixture) till it sprouts.

It has been suggested that the remedy came from Julius Caesar, who was known to be vain about his baldness.

The cosmetics book contained recipes for makeup made from ground minerals. Egyptians ground the black mineral galena and used it to darken and define their eyelids. They believed that thick eye makeup protected their eyes from the sun's glare and helped prevent eye disease caused by dust and flies. The eyeliner was a mix of powdered minerals and oil, which may have killed germs and insects' eggs. Egyptian women often colored their lips with ochre, a yellowish-red pigment, and stained their nails, palms, and the

Ancient coins mentioning Herod the Great

soles of their feet with henna, a natural reddish-brown dye. They also used it on their hair, while Greek women rubbed white lead powder into their hair and skin to lighten their complexions. Using extracts and juices from plants, such as seaweed and mulberry, women made different tints of rouges for their lips and cheeks.

Events beyond Egypt's borders continued to take up much of Cleopatra's time, however. After Antony had left, the young king of the small kingdom of Judaea came to visit Cleopatra. Eventually the young king would be known as Herod the Great, but he was in a desperate state when he called on Cleopatra. His tiny kingdom in what is today northern Israel had been invaded by the Parthians and Herod had barely managed to escape with his life. Aware of Cleopatra's relationship with Antony, he came to Alexandria to seek her help. Judaea had once belonged to the Ptolemies, and Cleopatra saw this as an opportunity to regain lost territory. She gave Herod a ship to sail to Italy, where he could try to win Antony's support against the Parthians.

It was a savvy move. Antony was looking for allies to fight Parthia. He was also in the midst of converting his eastern territories from provinces dominated by Roman governors into client-states ruled by local monarchs but still under Roman control. He hoped that the support of local leaders would help to quell rebellions against Roman rule. The Roman governors were notorious for their exploitation of their provinces and had often generated resistance and fomented trouble with their greed and corruption. Cicero had once written that, "Words cannot express . . . how bitterly we are hated among foreign nations because of the . . . outrageous conduct of the men whom we have sent to govern them." Antony seized on Herod as a useful ally and named him king of Judaea.

Antony now turned more of his attention to Parthia. He and his generals pushed the Parthians back, retaking the lands they had just conquered, including Syria and Judaea. They defeated a Roman renegade named Quintus Labienus, who had been aiding the Parthians, and also killed a strong Parthian prince named Pacorus. In the process they were able to recapture land as far east as the Euphrates River, pushing the Parthians back beyond their border. The victories were the cause of great rejoicing in Greece and Rome. Antony seemed poised to finally make the long dreamed of conquest.

Meanwhile, Octavian was having a difficult time fighting his own battles. He was attempting to get rid of the last of Pompey's sons, Sextus Pompey, who had become a notorious Roman outlaw and seized control of some of Rome's islands, including Sicily. In 38 B.C., Octavian asked Antony for assistance in dealing with Sextus, but when Antony arrived with his army, Octavian did not appear. He had tricked Antony into delaying his invasion of Parthia, which Octavian knew could bring his rival great success and glory. This was a typical ploy of the intelligent and wily Octavian, who knew he could never match Antony's prowess on the battlefield, or challenge his reputation among the soldiers, and would have to

Marcus Agrippa, Roman general and brilliant strategist, was a childhood friend of Octavian's. (Courtesy of Erich Lessing/Art Resource)

rely on his superior intelligence and cunning. Frustrated, Antony turned and sailed back to Athens, where he was preparing for the military campaign, a journey that took him several weeks.

Meanwhile, Octavian worked to restore some of the prestige he had lost because of his inability to defeat Sextus. His top commander, a loyal and formidable general

named Marcus Agrippa, put down a revolt in southwestern Gaul. Agrippa also moved Roman troops across the Rhine River in retaliation for attacks of Germanic tribes on Roman territory.

Relations between Antony and Octavian worsened. Although Octavia tried to smooth things over between her husband and her brother, Octavian always seemed to come out on top. While Octavian had some success fighting in the north, Sextus still menaced Rome. He had open negotiations with the Parthians about a possible alliance.

Once again, Octavian summoned Antony to ask for more assistance, and Antony returned to Italy with a fleet of three hundred ships. For the third time, Octavian failed to meet him. While waiting, Antony used the time in Rome to improve his political standing and to recruit soldiers. When he and Octavian finally met in 37 B.C., they signed another uneasy peace pact renewing the triumvirate for another five years.

As Antony returned yet again to Athens, he mulled over Octavian's insulting behavior. The younger man had repeatedly broken promises. Antony had given Octavian 130 ships after his desperate plea for help against Sextus, but he had not yet received the twenty thousand soldiers Octavian had promised in return.

As Octavian continued to withhold the promised legions, Antony grew more suspicious. He became convinced that Octavian intended on becoming the sole ruler of Rome, and that he could no longer trust him. The only way to compete with Octavian's growing influence and power was to win a spectacular military victory over Parthia.

Although Octavia appeared to be trying to soothe the relations between the two men, Antony no longer trusted his wife. While he had been married to her, his stature in Italy had declined and Octavian had seemed to always come out on top in negotiations. As Octavia accompanied Antony east to prepare for the campaign against Parthia, Octavia, who was pregnant, became ill. When their ship docked at the island of Corfu, Antony sent his wife back to Italy, and to her brother.

Antony sailed on east, toward Cleopatra. More than ever before he needed an ally. As soon as Antony arrived in Syria, he sent for Cleopatra, who, having not seen Antony in four years, came as quickly as she could.

Cleopatra traveled to Syria with their three-year-old twins, who had never seen their father. They met Antony in the city of Antioch on the eastern shores of the Mediterranean Sea. One of the largest cities in the east, Antioch was the ideal place for Antony to prepare for his invasion of Parthia.

seven

ISIS AND DIONYSUS REUNITED

Cleopatra and Antony spent the winter of 37–36 B.C. in Antioch. Their relationship continued to mix attraction with political ambition and necessity. Although they saw advantage in uniting forces against both the Parthians and Octavian, they drove hard bargains with each other. Cleopatra promised to finance Antony's campaign in Parthia. In return, Antony turned over a number of his eastern territories, including Sinai, the peninsula between the Mediterranean and Red Seas, Cyprus, highly valued for its cedar trees, which were used to build ships, parts of Crete, Phoenicia (modern day Lebanon), and Jordan, to Cleopatra.

Cleopatra wanted Judaea in order to have access to its valuable plantations of balsam shrubs, used in medicines and perfumes, and groves of date palms, which were said to be the best in the world. But Antony had already promised it to King Herod. Antony finally struck a complicated deal between Cleopatra and Herod in which Herod would retain his throne but pay rent to Cleopatra. Herod would also collect oil revenues from Malchus, the Arab king of Nabataene in northern Arabia, and turn them over to Cleopatra.

When the negotiations were over, Cleopatra ruled over many of the wealthiest cities in the East and owned valuable forests of timber that could supply a huge fleet of warships. She had expanded Egypt to nearly the greatest extent of any Ptolemaic ruler.

Romans viewed Antony's and Cleopatra's alliance with suspicion. Many thought that Cleopatra had played a role in Caesar's downfall by filling his head with ideas of becoming emperor, which was considered to be an "Eastern" idea, as

Mark Antony [left] *decorates the front of this Roman silver denarius, and Cleopatra VII graces the back.* (Courtesy of The Granger Collection)

was the tendency to closely identify with a specific god. The fear of an emperor convinced of his divinity was still a strong impulse in Roman politics. Now Antony had sent his pregnant Roman wife home and reunited sexually and politically with the Egyptian queen.

Antony seemed to pay little attention to how he was viewed back in Rome. After he and Cleopatra renewed their alliance they had coins minted picturing them together and inscribed with their names and titles—Cleopatra as queen and Antony as autocrator, or "absolute ruler" of the East. Although he remained a Roman triumvir in name, it looked more and more as though Antony was creating his own separate eastern empire with Cleopatra.

There was also concern about the expansion of Egypt Antony had granted to Cleopatra. Octavian and his supporters hinted that Antony had given away Roman territories that were not his to give away.

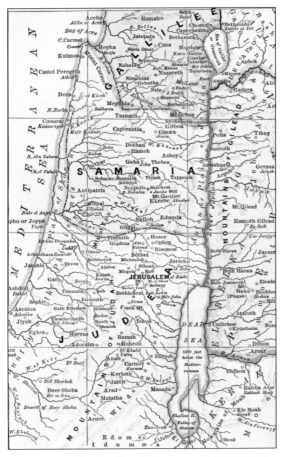

Ancient Israel (Courtesy of North Wind Picture Archives)

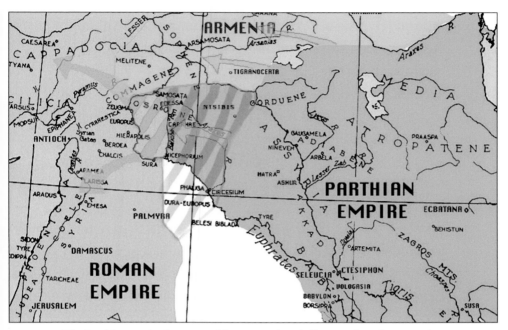

The Parthians took advantage of the uncertainty in Rome to launch an attack into Roman controlled areas.

In May of 36 B.C., Antony finally set off to defeat the Parthians. Cleopatra accompanied him for the first 150 miles, to the Euphrates River, which marked Rome's eastern frontier. As she turned back toward Antioch, Cleopatra was again pregnant with Antony's child. From Antioch, she traveled to Damascus, across the desert to the Sea of Galilee, and then south along the River Jordan to the city of Jericho, where she met King Herod, who invited her to Jerusalem. She took the opportunity to collect rent for her new properties in Judea.

In Jerusalem, she discovered that Herod's palace was filled with tension and intrigue. He had recently executed his uncle and his brother-in-law Aristobulus, whose mother,

Alexandra, was a close friend of Cleopatra's. Although Herod needed to remain on good terms with Antony, he resented the arrangement he'd been forced to make with Cleopatra. Years later, he claimed that Cleopatra had tried to seduce him during their talks, and that his friends had to dissuade him from having the Egyptian queen assassinated. While both of these stories might not have been true, they reveal how much hatred Cleopatra's power and ambition sometimes aroused.

When she got back to Alexandria, Cleopatra gave birth to another son she named Ptolemy Philadelphus, after Ptolemy II Philadelpus, the pharaoh who had extended Egypt to it largest extent during the Ptolemaic dynasty. Cleopatra now had three sons—Caesarion from Caesar, and Alexander Helios and Ptolemy Philadelphus from Antony. During this time, Cleopatra also learned Parthian, the language of the eastern domain she hoped to one day rule with Antony.

Recent events in Parthia encouraged Antony to continue his campaign there. The empire had fallen into confusion after its king, Orodes I, voluntarily abdicated his throne in 38 B.C., following the death of his son Pacorus in battle against Antony's generals. The king's next son, Phraates IV, murdered his father and thirty of his brothers in a bid for the throne and powerful Parthian leaders asked Antony for help in ousting Phraates.

Earlier Roman generals had failed to conquer Parthia. The Parthians were tough fighters and the rough, unfamiliar Parthian terrain had proven difficult. The Roman generals

A warrior executes a Parthian shot. This tomb decoration may be the earliest depiction of the fighting technique. (Courtesy of Werner Forman/Art Resource)

had to cross wide plains and deserts, which made it easy for skilled Parthian archers to pick them off.

One of their tactics became known as the "Parthian shot." Parthian horse archers would gallop away, as if in retreat, and then turn in their saddles and shoot backwards as accurately as if they had shot forward (this tactic is believed to be the origin of the expression "parting shot"). At the same time, the Parthians, for all of their agility in battle, lacked the Roman skill in hand-to-hand combat, and were inexperienced in siege warfare and had a hard time holding on to conquered territories, as Antony's speedy re-conquest of Syria attested.

Antony intended to avoid the mistakes of previous generals by taking the more difficult, but safer, northern route through mountain passes. This meant he would have to reach northern Parthia and take the Parthians by surprise before the onset of the harsh winter.

As Antony's army navigated the narrow, winding mountain trails, his men began to tire. Loaded down with large, heavy supply wagons laden with siege weapons such as stone throwers and battering rams, the journey to Parthia was long and trying. When Antony went ahead with the main army, the supply train was attacked and destroyed. King Artavasdes of Armenia, a former ally, had turned traitor and informed the Parthians of Antony's approach.

After the attack, Antony and his men attempted to regroup. They foraged for food and rebuilt their siege weapons. Whenever they stopped, though, raiding parties of Parthian horsemen rained arrows down on them and then quickly disappeared. Imminent winter storms and dwindling food supplies forced Antony to open negotiations with King Phraates, who agreed to allow Antony's men safe passage as long as they retreated to Syria. For twenty-seven days, they suffered attacks as they withdrew through Armenia, and King Phraates did not keep his word and Antony had to fight off repeated ambushes.

Cold mountain winds and diseases such as dysentery, a stomach infection caused by contaminated drinking water, ravaged the men. According to a remarkable (but probably embellished) story from Plutarch, a number of them perished after eating a certain wild root:

He that had eaten of this root remembered nothing in the world, and employed himself only in moving great stones from one place to another, which he did with as much earnestness and industry as if it had been a business of the greatest consequence, and thus through all the camp there was nothing to be seen but men grubbing upon the ground at stones, which they carried from place to place, until in the end they vomited and died.

Before it was over, Antony lost twenty thousand men, nearly half of his troops. His soldiers largely remained loyal, though. He had shared their hardships and tried to reassure his men. As they sickened and died he traveled from tent to tent offering "his sympathies with the wounded and attending to their wants," wrote Plutarch.

When the exhausted, depleted army finally limped into Syria, Antony sent word for Cleopatra to bring him supplies. In January of 35 B.C., she returned to Antioch with winter clothing, supplies, and wages. But this re-union between the Roman general and the Egyptian queen was not as joyful as their previous one. A devastated and ashamed Antony drank himself into a stupor while waiting for Cleopatra. When she finally arrived, they returned to Alexandria to plan their revenge on Armenia's traitorous King Artavasdes.

In Rome, Octavian seized upon Antony's defeat to spread rumors about the couple. He insinuated that Antony had failed because he was more concerned with returning to

Cleopatra than with conquering Rome's longtime enemy. Octavian also devised a clever way to further sully Antony's reputation. Under the guise of helping Antony with the Parthian war, he sent seventy ships, which were of little value in the landlocked conflict with Parthia, and two thousand soldiers, a pittance compared to the twenty thousand Octavian had once promised. Octavian sent Octavia, Antony's spurned wife, as a pawn to deliver the offensively small gift. He surmised that Antony would reject his wife, further damaging his reputation as a husband and a Roman.

Antony reacted exactly as Octavian had

Octavian was only eighteen years old when thrust into Roman politics by Caesar's assassination. His rivals often underestimated his abilities and cunning.

planned. When Octavia reached Athens, she received a letter from Antony to send the ships on to him but she was to return to Rome. Octavia dutifully returned to her husband's house in Rome and offered no complaint against Antony. Inevitably, she was extolled as the perfect wife and mother, noble in the disgrace caused by Antony's preference for his exotic foreign mistress.

Antony responded with reminders about Octavian's broken promises, such as the promised troops and ships Octavian had never sent. When Octavian called Cleopatra a harlot, Antony criticized Octavian's own sexual conduct, citing his numerous affairs. "Is your wife the only woman you take to bed?" Antony bluntly asked.

A year later, in 34 B.C., Antony set off to deal with King Artavasdes, whose betrayal had undermined the Parthian campaign. He quickly conquered the kingdom and brought the king back to Alexandria as a prisoner. In Alexandria, Antony staged a magnificent triumph commemorating his victory. Antony and Cleopatra reintroduced the Order of the Inimitable Livers. During the revels, Cleopatra and Antony, garbed as Isis-Aphrodite and Dionysus-Osiris respectively, sat on golden thrones high above the crowds while their children sat on smaller silver thrones.

When King Artavasdes was brought before Cleopatra and told to address her as a goddess, he refused. In a Roman triumph, Artavasdes would surely have been put to death, but Cleopatra and Antony decided to spare his life. He and his family were held as prisoners in Alexandria.

Several days after the parade, Antony bestowed new territories on Cleopatra's children. Antony named Caesarion as king of Egypt, to rule jointly with his mother. He publicly proclaimed that Caesarion was Caesar's legitimate heir, insinuating that Octavian was a usurper. Six-year-old Alexander Helios was betrothed to the daughter of the king of Media and declared the future king of Armenia, Media, and Parthia, although Parthia had yet to be conquered. Antony wanted an alliance with the Median king as a bulwark against a Parthian invasion in case war broke out between Antony and Octavian. Alexander Helios's twin, Cleopatra, was made the future queen of Crete and of Cyrene. Antony's youngest son, two-year-old Ptolemy Philadelphus, received northern Syria and parts of Macedonia.

To Cleopatra, these ceremonies, which became known in the Mediterranean world as the "Donations of Alexandria," were the beginning of a new dynasty. Antony was repaying her for her allegiance and support. In return, she recognized him as her fellow divine ruler.

Romans saw things differently. As news of the festivities filtered back into Italy, the outrage was widespread. Triumphs had traditionally only been held in Rome. By staging the celebration in Alexandria, Antony seemed to suggest that the Egyptian city was now Rome's equal. To Romans, the "Donations of Alexandria" were a threat to Roman supremacy in the Mediterranean world.

Meanwhile, Octavian had made himself increasingly popular in Rome. He took a page out of Antony and Cleopatra's book and depicted himself as a god. But rather

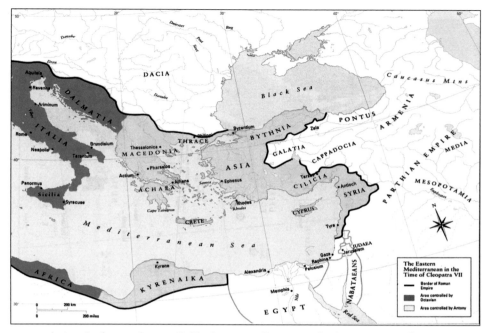

Antony's plans on how to divide the eastern Roman territories were not well received in Rome.

than Dionysus, Octavian chose Apollo—Dionysus's foil and the god of light, healing, music, and the sun. In 35 B.C. he finally defeated Sextus Pompey and now Sicily was available for the taking. When the third triumvir, Lepidus, ill-advisedly, moved to annex Sicily to his North African territory, Octavian pounced. He captured Sicily and deposed Lepidus, confiscating his territory and troops without ever consulting Antony. The triumvirate was no more.

Now only Antony blocked Octavian from total control over Rome. Octavian realized most Romans would not support another civil war, but he knew if he could convince them that Cleopatra was the real enemy, he would have no trouble getting support. He began to engineer a war against the foreign queen. He cast Cleopatra as an evil seductress who had ensnared the formerly noble Antony with her

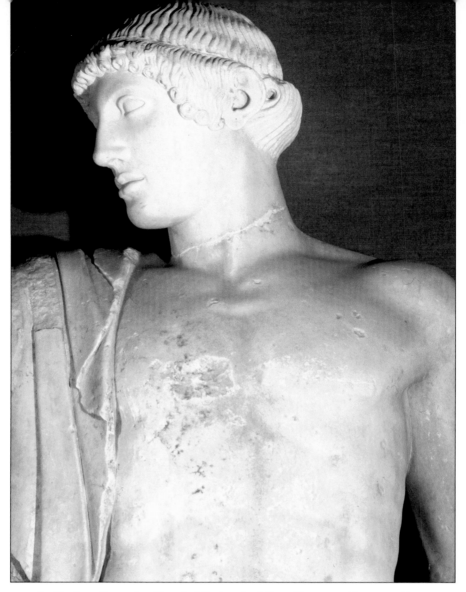

Apollo, from the west pediment of the temple of Zeus (Courtesy of Borromeo/Art Resource)

sexual charms and won him to her goal of building an Egyptian empire to rival, and possibly even subjugate, Rome. Cleopatra, he said, was delirious with dreams of fortune and power and filled with a hatred of Rome. First she had seduced Julius Caesar to this purpose, and now she had swept up Antony in her evil scheme.

eight

WAR WITH ROME

Cleopatra and Antony spent the winter of 33–32 B.C. in Ephesus, a Roman seaport at the mouth of the Cayster River on the Aegean Sea. They worked to get ready for the coming fight with Octavian, busily recruiting soldiers and support from surrounding kingdoms. They amassed five hundred ships built in Alexandria, seventy-five thousand Roman soldiers, and nearly sixty thousand more from Syria, Greece, and other parts of Asia Minor.

Despite his spreading of rumors, Octavian had not yet openly denounced Antony. However, their feud became

public when Octavian denounced Antony to the Senate, after another senator praised Antony. Nearly one third of the Roman Senate, and both consuls, who still supported Antony and believed he was interested in restoring the republic to its glory, traveled to Ephesus and joined Antony.

Antony claimed he wasn't interested in power, and only wanted to stop Octavian from becoming emperor. Somewhat contrarily, he also supported Caesarion, though Caesar's heir had no legitimate place in the Republic.

Soon after the Roman senators arrived at Ephesus, several of them began to grumble about Cleopatra's presence at Antony's side during war councils and formal dinners. They had hoped to negotiate a reconciliation between Antony and Octavian and saw discarding the unpopular Cleopatra and returning to Octavia as necessary. They advised Antony to send Cleopatra back to Alexandria, but a few spoke up on her behalf, citing her intelligence and contributions to the war effort, and yet another group suggested he have her murdered and claim Egypt for himself.

Cleopatra was worried Antony would try to be rid of her. She even bribed one of Antony's leading generals, Publius Canidus Crassus, to plead her case. "I do not see to which of the kings who have joined this expedition Cleopatra is inferior in wisdom," Canidus dutifully told Antony, "for she has for a long time governed by herself a vast kingdom, and has learnt in your company the handling of great affairs." In any case, Antony was convinced he could not afford to wage war without her.

Cleopatra and Antony moved their headquarters to Samos, the easternmost island in the Aegean Sea. For days, Antony drank and celebrated the beginning of a war he felt sure he would win:

> This one island for many days resounded with the music of flutes and harps. The theaters were filled, and choruses competed against one another. Every city sent an ox for sacrifice and kings vied with one another in entertainments and gifts. Everywhere men began to ask how on earth the conquerors would celebrate their victory when their festivities at the opening of the war were so expensive.

From Samos, they moved on to Athens, where Antony indulged in more drinking, arranged more festivities, and was hailed again as the New Dionysus. Cleopatra urged him to make a final break from Octavian, and in June of 32 B.C., Antony formally announced his divorce from Octavia.

Roman law prohibited marriage to more than one person. While Cleopatra and Antony lived as though they were husband and wife, no one knows for sure if they ever married. Some sources refer to Cleopatra as Antony's mistress, others—including a letter by Antony himself—called her his wife. In Egypt they were considered a divinely married couple represented by the god Dionysus and the goddess Isis, which was enough to give their children legitimacy.

Divorcing Octavia was the final break with Octavian that Antony had intended it to be, but it also prompted several

Antony and Cleopatra (Courtesy of The Granger Collection)

senators to desert him. They returned to Italy with gossipy tales about Antony and Cleopatra's extravagant behavior, including stories of Antony massaging Cleopatra's feet at state banquets and his interrupting business meetings to read love notes from her.

One of the senators also told Octavian that Antony's will was in Rome. Octavian seized the will and read parts of it aloud to the Senate. Although it may have been forged by

Octavian, it had a dramatic impact. The will declared that Cleopatra's children would be Antony's heirs, and stipulated that he wished to be buried in Alexandria next to her. In doing so, Octavian aroused suspicions that Antony planned to move the capital from Rome to Alexandria.

Octavian gradually convinced Rome of Antony's treacherous behavior, but he also put the blame on Cleopatra. Antony, he said, was like a drugged, entranced man and this view made it into the accounts of many ancient chroniclers. "He gave not a thought to honor," wrote the Roman historian Dio Cassius, "but became the Egyptian woman's slave and devoted his time to his passion for her. This caused him to do many outrageous things."

Octavian also sought to cast Cleopatra as a monster out to destroy the entire Roman Empire. Cleopatra and "her vile gang of sick, polluted creatures, / crazed with hope and drunk with her past successes / was planning the death and destruction of the empire," wrote the Roman poet Horace.

The Egyptian queen, by Octavian's account, had lured Antony away from his decent Roman wife. Now she was also forcing him to act against Rome:

> Who would not tear his hair at the sight of Roman soldiers serving as bodyguards of the queen? Who would not weep when he sees and hears what Antony has become? He has abandoned his whole ancestral way of life, has embraced alien and barbaric customs. And to crown it all, he bestows gifts of whole islands and parts of continents as though he were master of the entire earth and sea.

Horace, Roman poet (Courtesy of The Granger Collection)

Antony and Cleopatra's army occupied several bases on islands along the western coast of Greece. They faced Italy along the Ionian Sea, which lies between Italy and Greece. The bulk of their fleet, however, was tucked away in the well-protected Gulf of Ambracia, behind the small seaport of Actium.

While Cleopatra and Antony's force was larger than Octavian's, it was not of the same caliber. Unable to recruit troops in Italy, they had supplemented their land army with inexperienced men from the East. Their naval fleet, although larger, was made up primarily of large galleys called quinqueremes that, as it turned out, Agrippa's smaller, more nimble vessels, called Liburnians, were able to outmaneuver. Octavian and Agrippa's navy was also better seasoned and in top form after their recent battles against Sextus and his pirates.

Octavian's supporters publicized omens of Antony and Cleopatra's downfall. One of Antony's statues was reportedly sighted sweating blood, while another blew over in strong winds and smashed to pieces. When children in the streets of Rome acted out the coming war, Octavian was always the winner.

The principle locations leading up to the battle at Actium

The Battle of Actium has captured the imagination of artists for 2,000 years.
(Courtesy of The Granger Collection)

As Antony and Cleopatra prepared for battle, Agrippa made his move. His strategy was to attack each of Antony's scattered forces one at a time, taking advantage of Antony's decision to spread his troops throughout southwestern Greece. In March of 31 B.C., Agrippa captured Methone, Antony and Cleopatra's southernmost naval base. Soon their second fleet fell at Corfu, followed by Agrippa's capture of one outpost after another. Eventually, Antony's supply route from Egypt was cut off. Meanwhile, Octavian landed his army on Greece's mainland and set up camp north of the opening to the gulf, opposite Antony and Cleopatra's camp at Actium.

As the summer wore on, Antony and Cleopatra began to realize they were trapped in the Gulf of Ambracia. Agrippa's fleet blocked the entrance, which was only a half-mile wide, and the southern supply routes, while an army commanded by Octavian menaced them from the north. Food and supplies became short, and malaria and dysentery spread through the army, which was encamped in a swampy, mosquito-infested area. As Antony's ranks thinned because of disease, his ships were attacked by wood-eating worms. Soldiers began deserting or defecting to Octavian's camp, where they told of Antony's plight.

Antony attempted to break the blockade of enemy ships, but failed. Next he tried to draw Octavian into a land battle, but Octavian wisely refused to leave his protected hilltop encampment and waited for Agrippa to defeat Antony at sea.

Their poor fortune and Antony's heavy drinking strained relations between him and Cleopatra. A false story circulated that Cleopatra planned to poison Antony. He became suspicious and refused to touch his food or drink unless a condemned criminal tasted it first. Cleopatra decided to teach Antony a lesson and at the same time prove her loyalty. One night she filled her wine goblet from the wine jar from which he had been drinking. She drank from the cup, dipped a wreath of flowers from her hair into it, and then handed it to Antony. He lifted the cup to his lips, but Cleopatra dashed the goblet from his hands, saying that the wine was poisoned. When he replied that she had just drunk from the same cup, she told him the wreath was

A modern photo of the Gulf of Ambracia

poisoned. Cleopatra pointed out that she could have killed him at any time.

By August, Antony and his generals had come up with two possible escape routes. According to one plan, they could abandon their fleet of ships and retreat inland over the mountains into eastern Greece. Antony's commander, Canidus, argued for this retreat because Antony excelled at inland battles. Canidus, who earlier had persuaded Antony not to send Cleopatra back to Egypt, had come to think she was doing him more harm than help. He told Antony that if they drew Octavian into a land battle, and if she was sent back to Egypt, Octavian would have to acknowledge that his war was against Antony, not Cleopatra. Antony finally agreed to ask Cleopatra to go back to Egypt, but she refused.

Cleopatra also argued strenuously against abandoning the fleet. Most of her treasure was hidden in her flagship. She said it was suicide to take the weakened army over treacherous mountain passes. Even if the soldiers survived the journey, they would probably be cut off from their supply base in Egypt. A retreat would also cause panic and further desertions. Cleopatra pushed another plan—to fight their way out of the harbor by ship and escape to Egypt, where they could regroup.

As the fighting wore on, Antony's outnumbered and demoralized oarsmen had a hard time using the large, unwieldy quinqueremes to their advantage. The ships were designed for powerful, head-on attacks and could not keep up with Agrippa's smaller, more maneuverable ships. "Octavian's ships resembled cavalry, now launching a charge, and now retreating, since they could attack or draw off as they chose, while Antony's were like heavy infantry, warding off the enemy's efforts to ram them," wrote Dio Cassius.

Cleopatra held back with her sixty ships and watched as Antony drew Agrippa's ships to the north, away from her, before slowly sailing west. When Cleopatra's ships raised their sails and headed south to the open sea, Antony switched to a smaller, faster vessel and followed her. Octavian's supporters later claimed that he abandoned his troops to be with his mistress, or had planned to flee with her all along. Others speculate that, realizing the battle was lost, he gave the command for his other ships to follow him to Egypt but they refused. By the next morning Agrippa had captured or sunk all of Antony's remaining fleet.

Antony and Cleopatra had escaped with their lives and about one hundred of their ships, including her treasure ship. What they did not know was that their land army, which had for so long been Antony's strong suit, had vanished. Hemmed in by Octavian's soldiers, the men were offered generous terms of land and money for their surrender and had abandoned Antony.

Antony was crushed by his loss at the Battle of Actium. His power and prestige were gone. It appeared to many that he had deserted his men, and he began to contemplate suicide.

Cleopatra sailed ahead to Alexandra. Afraid her subjects might revolt if they heard of the disastrous defeat, she sailed into her home harbor with flags waving and triumphant songs playing. As soon as she was safe, though, she began killing anyone she suspected of betrayal.

In the meantime Antony, took what remained of his own fleet to Paraetonium, about one hundred miles west of Alexandria on Egypt's Mediterranean coast, where he first learned that his legions in North Africa had defected to Octavian's camp. He tried to commit suicide, but was stopped by two of his advisers.

He returned to Alexandria, and moved into a small house near the Pharos lighthouse. He called the house Timonium, after Timon of Athens, a famous Greek nobleman and misanthrope who lived in solitude. Soon, his general Canidus arrived with the news that rest of his army had deserted him. Despondent, he refused to speak to anyone, even Cleopatra.

Timon and Apemantus, from Timon of Athens *by William Shakespeare*
(Courtesy of Bridgeman Art Library)

nine

THE SNAKE STRIKES

News of Cleopatra and Antony's defeat at the Battle of
Actium spread quickly. Over the last months of 31 B.C.,
most of their remaining allies deserted them. The rulers
in Greece, Asia Minor, North Africa, and Judaea swore allegiance to Octavian. Herod, who owed Antony his crown
and his kingdom, joined the defectors after traveling to
Alexandria and unsuccessfully trying to persuade Antony
to assassinate Cleopatra.

Cleopatra and Antony waited in Alexandria for the
inevitable Roman invasion, which Octavian had to delay
because the soldiers who had fought for him in his campaigns against Sextus and Antony were demanding their

wages and release from service. The wave of discontent caused by the expensive war began to create tension in Rome because taxes had to be increased to pay for Octavian's army.

Octavian was forced to return to Rome to deal with the tension. The delay gave Cleopatra time to gather new forces in Egypt. However, the unrest in Rome made an attack on Egypt inevitable. Octavian could not raise any more money from taxes, and the only way to pay his soldiers was to conquer Egypt and seize its treasury.

Cleopatra resolved to fight to the end. It was victory or death. Newly filled with energy, she began building ships and recruiting forces. To rally public support, she staged grand festivities celebrating the coming of age of her oldest son Caesarion. Now sixteen, many hoped Caesarion would live up to his father's legacy. Unfortunately, these festivities also emphasized the threat Cleopatra's son posed to Octavian.

With Antony's legions fast abandoning him, Cleopatra had to find other allies in the East. She sent Caesarion and his tutor Rhodon, as well as part of the royal treasure, up the Nile to Coptos in Upper Egypt. From Coptos they would be able to reach a port on the Red Sea and set sail for India and hopefully find new allies there. Cleopatra also strengthened her pact with the kingdom of Media, where the king's infant daughter was already betrothed to her son, Alexander Helios. Media was an enemy of both Parthia and Parthia's occasional ally, Armenia. As a gesture of goodwill, Cleopatra executed King Artavasdes,

Cleopatra and an adult Caesarion make offerings to the goddess Hathor on the back of her temple in Dendera, Egypt. Caesarion's headpiece represents his kingship over both Upper and Lower Egypt.

the Armenian king whose life had been spared after the triumph in Alexandria, and sent his head to the court in Media. An alliance with both India and Media would encircle Parthia.

These were ambitious plans that required moving ships from the Mediterranean to the Red Sea. Although a canal linking the two seas had been built near Suez centuries before, it had fallen into disrepair and was blocked by sand in places. Undeterred, Cleopatra had the vessels raised onto wooden frames with rollers and pulled overland for more than twenty miles to Heroonpolis, near the Gulf of Suez. However, when the ships arrived, they were burned by Malchus, the Arab king who was still bitter over the rent arrangements that had been made between Cleopatra and Herod. Cleopatra avenged her loss by having Malchus murdered, but the damage was done.

Each day the news grew worse. As Octavian gained momentum, more and more of Antony's men, many of whom had fought with him for years, defected. Antony generously released any soldiers who wanted to leave and paid them their due. Soon his former legions were gathered against him under one of Octavian's generals, Cornelius Gallus. Soon it was clear that Cleopatra and Antony had only two options. They could defend Alexandria or negotiate with Octavian.

Cleopatra tried to open negotiations with Octavian. She sent generous gifts and even agreed to give up her crown if Octavian would allow her children to rule Egypt. While Octavian gladly accepted her gifts, he gave evasive answers to her entreaties and tried to persuade her to kill Antony. Antony's son, Antyllus, went to Octavian with a large bribe and a promise from Antony to retire from public life. Antony even offered to kill himself if doing so would save Cleopatra. But Octavian, who by now had amassed an army in Syria and was marching toward Egypt, saw no reason to seriously negotiate.

Antony, who had grown increasingly dissolute, finally pulled himself together. He moved back to the palace with Cleopatra, where they held feasts and festivities and grimly renamed their old circle of friends the "Order of the Inseparable in Death." They decided to have fun until they either escaped or died.

Despite this outward show of bravery, Cleopatra was preoccupied with thoughts of death. She had a resplendent mausoleum built to house her tomb, and supposedly collected different kinds of deadly poisonous animals and tested them out on condemned criminals in search of the best one to use when the time came to commit suicide. It is possible that the stories of her preparing for death were more Roman propaganda, intended to illustrate her excessiveness and cruelty.

Frustrated by Octavian's unwillingness to negotiate, Antony lashed out. He seized Octavian's emissary, a freedman named Thyrus, had the man beaten, and sent him back to Octavian with a message. "The man's inquisitive, impertinent ways, provoked me," he wrote, "and in my circumstances I cannot be expected to be very patient. But if it offend you, you have got my freedman, Hipparchus, with you; hang him up and whip him to make us even." The offer was a taunt—Hipparchus had previously defected to Octavian.

By the summer of 30 B.C., Octavian had captured the port of Pelusium and was nearing Alexandria. He sent a group of cavalry ahead, but Antony gathered his troops and routed them on the outskirts of the city. It was a minor victory, but when he returned to Alexandria, Antony presented one of his bravest soldiers to Cleopatra, who gave the man a golden helmet and breastplate. The next day, the soldier fled the city to join Octavian.

Desperate for a way out, Antony even challenged Octavian to a duel, one man against the other. Although Antony was nearly twice Octavian's age, hand-to-hand combat was not Octavian's strength and he rejected the offer, wryly pointing out that Antony "might find several other ways of ending his life." Antony attempted to bribe enemy soldiers to come to his side, but none of them accepted.

Antony and Cleopatra's only option was to fight with their dwindling forces. The night before what they thought was likely to be their last battle, Cleopatra and Antony dined with friends. Antony told them he no longer counted on victory and only hoped for an honorable death. He ate and drank heavily, as though this were to be his last dinner. Some of his soldiers and friends wept to hear him talk so dejectedly.

According to legend, that night at midnight people heard the sounds of various musical instruments playing and of voices singing. The music sounded like a troop of revelers singing and dancing wildly through the streets and at the outer gate to the city, which led to the enemy camp, the noise swelled and then suddenly stopped. Many Alexandrians took the sounds as an omen. According to tradition, the gods would forsake a city before it fell, and they whispered that the sounds came from Antony's favorite god, Dionysus, the god of revels, leaving the city.

Early the next day, August 1, Antony's remaining ships sailed into the harbor to confront Octavian. But instead of fighting, they surrendered without a battle and then doubled back toward Alexandria to join the attack with Octavian's fleet. The battle was over, and Antony's defeat was complete.

Convinced Cleopatra had orchestrated the mass defections in order to save herself, Antony rushed into the palace, crying "Cleopatra has betrayed me," but the men had abandoned Antony because their odds of survival were much greater with Octavian. Soon the Roman army entered Alexandria and approached the royal palace.

By the time Antony reached the palace, Cleopatra had fled. She and two of her servants locked themselves inside her new, huge mausoleum. She ordered her servants to hide the royal treasure in the mausoleum's storeroom. The treasure was her last bargaining chip to convince Octavian to spare her children's lives. Cleopatra's servants heaped wood and flammable materials all around the treasure. She was prepared to burn it all if Octavian would not bargain.

Possibly because of Cleopatra's retreat to her tomb, the rumor spread that she had committed suicide. When Antony received the false message that Cleopatra was dead, he asked his servant, Eros, to kill him too. Eros obediently drew his sword, but then, unable to kill his master, turned it upon himself and died at Antony's feet. "Well done, Eros," said Antony, "you were not able to do it yourself, but you teach me what I must do." Antony then grabbed another sword and plunged it into his own stomach, dropped the weapon, and staggered to the ground. The bleeding soon slowed, however, leaving Antony writhing on the ground, begging someone to finish him off. Then a messenger arrived to tell him Cleopatra still lived.

News of Antony's mortal wound spread. Cleopatra ordered two of her servants to bring Antony to her mausoleum. Getting Antony inside would be difficult. Cleopatra would not open the heavy, well-barricaded doors, for fear that her servants would not have time to shut and rebolt them if Octavian's men reached the mausoleum. Instead, the two servants lowered ropes from one of the unfinished upper windows to two servants outside, who tied the ropes around the dying Antony. Cleopatra and her two servants then managed to hoist him up through the window.

It was later written that Cleopatra sobbed with grief at the sight of her dying lover. After lowering him onto a couch, she tried to stitch his wound, but it was no use. Antony called for some wine to ease his pain, and then, stretching out his arms toward Cleopatra, asked her not to pity him. He had, "fallen not ignobly, a Roman by a Roman overcome," as Plutarch wrote. He died in Cleopatra's arms.

In legends, Antony died in Cleopatra's arms. (Library of Congress)

Soon after Antony stabbed himself, one of his body-guards had seized his bloodstained sword, slipped away to the enemy camp, and informed Octavian of Antony's suicide attempt. Octavian sent one of his trusted officers, Proculeius, to arrest Cleopatra at the mausoleum and to prevent her from destroying the treasure.

Cleopatra refused to unbolt the doors, but spoke to Proculeius through the door. She told him of Antony's death and asked to negotiate directly with Octavian. In the course of their conversation, Proculeius noticed the open window through which Cleopatra's servants had hauled Antony.

When Proculeius told Octavian that Antony was dead, Octavian wept, like Julius Caesar had wept upon learning of Pompey's death. Proculeius also told Octavian about the open window, and then returned to the mausoleum with Cornelius Gallus, the general who had occupied North Africa and who had arrived with his troops in Alexandria.

While Gallus distracted the queen by speaking through the closed door of the mausoleum, Proculeius climbed a ladder to the open window, crawled past Antony's body and reached the top of the stairs behind Cleopatra and her servants, who were talking to Gallus at the doorway. When one of Cleopatra's servants spotted Proculeius and cried out to Cleopatra, the queen reached for a dagger she had hidden in her dress to use to kill herself. But Proculeius pounced on her and wrestled the dagger from her grasp. Cleopatra was a prisoner of Rome.

In the meantime, Octavian marched triumphantly into Alexandria. He had the Alexandrian philosopher Areius Didymus at his side to show that he would be fair to the conquered city. But, in private, he ordered several executions, including those of Canidus, Antony's top general, and Antyllus, his son with Fulvia.

Antony's body was buried in a tomb near Cleopatra's mausoleum, and she was allowed to attend his funeral. She then took up residence, under heavy guard, in a room in her mausoleum. For several days she refused to eat. It was rumored that she was shamed and scared by the thought of being forced to march through the streets of Rome as her sister Arsinoë had years before. Supposedly, she repeated the phrase "I'll never go in triumph" over and over.

Cleopatra spent about in week in confinement before Octavian met with her. She asked for mercy for her children, but Octavian refused to grant it. He also announced his plans to annex Egypt and hold a triumph in Rome.

Some historians argue that Octavian hoped Cleopatra would commit suicide, and by revealing his plans, he hoped to encourage her to do so. If she killed herself, he wouldn't be accused of cruelty for killing the defeated queen.

Cleopatra asked to visit Antony's tomb. Octavian granted her permission and she laid some flowers on Antony's grave. She then sent a letter to Octavian asking to be buried at Antony's side before returning to the mausoleum.

On August 12, 30 B.C., Cleopatra bathed and dressed herself as the goddess Isis, ate a sumptuous last meal, and lay down on a golden couch, and died.

When Octavian read Cleopatra's letter he knew she intended suicide. He sent men to her chambers, but she was dead when they arrived. Her hairdresser, Iras, lay dead at her feet and her lady-in-waiting, Charmion, stood unsteadily beside the body, adjusting the Egyptian crown that sat atop Cleopatra's head. Seeing the spectacle, one of Octavian's men angrily cried out to Charmion, "A fine deed, this, Charmion." To which Cleopatra's lady-in-waiting responded, "Indeed, most fine. And right for the descendant of so many kings," and fell over dead.

No one knows for sure how Cleopatra killed herself. There were no dagger marks or blood, so she must have

Octavian visits Cleopatra. (Library of Congress)

used poison. Some think the poison was hidden in a hairpin. At the time of her death, it was said that she had used a cobra, or Egyptian asp, that had been smuggled in to her in a basket of figs by a loyal friend or servant. The Roman soldiers who found her claimed that two faint traces of fang-like puncture wounds were visible on her arm. Though no snake was found in the palace, some said they saw tracks of one in the sand of the nearby beach. The sacred hooded cobra, called the *Naja haja,* was considered in Egypt to be a symbol of royalty, Isis, and everlasting life. It was not unusual for people to die of snakebites and it was even a common method of execution. The snake's bite caused drowsiness, then coma, followed by a painless death.

With the death of the thirty-nine year old Egyptian queen, Egypt's Ptolemaic dynasty came to an end. For nearly three hundred years she and her ancestors had ruled Egypt and extended Egyptian influence throughout the Mediterranean region, western Asia, and deep into Africa and Arabia.

In the wake of Cleopatra's death, some Romans considered her behavior brave. The Roman poet Horace, who

Charmion, Cleopatra's defiant maid, adjusts the dead queen's crown before dying herself. (Library of Congress)

before had called her a drunken madwoman, even held her up as a model of courage and determination:

> Yet she preferred a finer style of dying:
> She did not, like a woman, shirk the dagger
> or seek by speed at sea
> To change her Egypt for obscurer shores,
>
> But gazing on her desolated palace
> With a calm smile, unflinchingly laid hand on
> The angry asps until
> Her veins had drunk the deadly poison deep:
>
> And, death determined, fiercer then than ever,
> Perished. Was she to grace a haughty triumph,
> Dethroned . . .? Not Cleopatra.

In her death, Cleopatra was fortunately spared the news of the fate of her eldest son. Octavian saw Caesarion as a threat to his power. "It is bad to have too many Caesars," as Areius Didymus observed. When Caesarion's tutor betrayed their whereabouts in Upper Egypt, Octavian had Caesarion murdered.

Antony and Cleopatra's other children were not harmed. Cleopatra Selene and Alexander Helios were forced to march in Octavian's triumph in Rome behind an effigy of Cleopatra, depicted in her golden couch with snakes twirled around an arm. They were taken in by Octavia, Antony's ex-wife. When Cleopatra Selene grew up, she was married to Prince Juba II of the North African province of Numidia, part of modern day Tunisia. The fates

A sculpture of Roman emperor Augustus, the former triumvir Octavian
(Courtesy of Scala/Art Resource)

of Alexander Helios and young Ptolemy Philadelphus are unknown.

Although Octavian made Egypt a Roman province later in 30 B.C., he was careful to treat Cleopatra's memory with outward respect. Cleopatra's statues were left standing, but Octavian tore down all statues of Antony and recalled all currency bearing his image.

Cleopatra's treasury went to Rome. Octavian used it to buy land to reward his soldiers. Egypt became an important and lucrative Roman province.

Michelangelo's Cleopatra (Courtesy of Scala/Art Resource)

Octavian ruled Rome for more than forty years. He eventually became the first emperor of the Roman Empire, taking the honorary name Augustus. The month of Octavian's final victory over Antony and Cleopatra was named August in his honor, and the preceding month was named July for Julius Caesar. The Roman Empire would eventually cover land now occupied by thirty countries from Morocco to the borders of Scotland, Romania, Egypt, and Syria.

For centuries, Romans considered Cleopatra to have been a dangerous woman and treacherous enemy. Historians loyal to the empire besmirched her reputation, purged records of her life, and spread tales of her greed and immorality. This account by the Roman historian Josephus is typical:

> There was no lawless deed which she did not commit; she had already caused the death by poisoning of her brother when he was only fifteen years old because she knew that he was to become king, and she had her sister Arsinoë killed. . . . In sum, nothing was enough by itself for this extravagant woman, who was enslaved by her appetites, so that the whole world failed to satisfy the desires of her imagination.

Cleopatra's story has inspired many artists and authors. Michelangelo drew her with snakes entwined in her hair and hundreds of other paintings have depicted her death throes. William Shakespeare's play *Antony and Cleopatra* dramatized her story. Even today, Cleopatra is a popular subject for playwrights and film directors. She has been played in films by such glamorous actresses as Vivien Leigh and Elizabeth Taylor.

Cleopatra is one of the most famous queens to ever to have lived, but her life is not well documented. Only fifty papyri dated to her reign have been uncovered. To this day whether she was ruthless and immoral, or dedicated and brave, depends on who is writing her history. Regardless, she remains a constantly intriguing and alluring figure, unlikely to be forgotten.

timeline

70 or 69 B.C.	Cleopatra is born. Mother dies shortly after.
58 B.C.	Father, Ptolemy XII, requests military help from Rome to quell mobs in Alexandria.
57 B.C.	Sister Berenice seizes Egyptian throne.
55 B.C.	Roman troops help restore Ptolemy XII to power; Berenice is executed.
51 B.C.	Ptolemy XII dies; Cleopatra and half brother Ptolemy XIII become joint rulers of Egypt.
49 B.C.	Exiled by Ptolemy XIII and his advisors, flees to Syria.
48 B.C.	Roman civil war between Caesar and Pompey; restored to throne with help from Caesar; Ptolemy XIII drowns in battle; Cleopatra rules jointly with Ptolemy XIV.
47 B.C.	Gives birth to son with Caesar, Caesarion.
46 B.C.	Travels to Rome as Caesar's guest.
44 B.C.	Caesar is murdered; Cleopatra returns to Egypt; Ptolemy XIV dies.

42 B.C.	Mark Antony, Caius Octavius, and Marcus Lepidus form Second Triumvirate, defeat Caesar's assassins.
41 B.C.	Meets Antony at Tarsus.
40 B.C.	Gives birth to twins with Antony.
36 B.C.	Antony's attack on Parthians fails; Triumvirate crumbles; gives birth to third child with Antony.
34 B.C.	Receives gifts of land and titles from Antony in "Donations of Alexandria."
32 B.C.	Octavian declares war on Cleopatra.
31 B.C.	Defeated at Battle of Actium.
30 B.C.	Octavian invades Egypt; Antony dies; Cleopatra commits suicide on August 12.

Sources

CHAPTER ONE: The Seventh Cleopatra

p. 30, "No one has . . ." Michael Grant, *Cleopatra* (London: Phoenix Press, 2000), 35.

p. 35, "because I am . . ." Stanley Burstein, *The Reign of Cleopatra* (Westport, CT: Greenwood Press, 2004), 47.

CHAPTER TWO: The Shadow of Rome

p. 42, "They vomit . . ." Ibid., 61.

p. 46, "friend and ally . . ." Grant, *Cleopatra,* 13.

p. 53, "And while Rome . . ." Polly Schoyer Brooks, *Cleopatra: Goddess of Egypt, Enemy of Rome* (New York: Harper Collins, 1995), 5.

CHAPTER FOUR: Murder in Rome

p. 74, "would have sailed . . ." Hughes-Hallett, *Histories, Dreams, and Distortions,* 76.

p. 82, "*Veni, vidi, vici* . . ." Brooks, *Goddess of Egypt, Enemy of Rome*, 46.

p. 83, "Those fools think . . ." Ibid., 48

p. 87, "Men ought to look . . ." Arthur Weigall, *The Life and Times of Cleopatra, Queen of Egypt* (New York: G. P. Putnam's Sons/The Knickerbocker Press, 1924), 175.

p. 90, "Tyranny must end . . ." Brooks, 55.

p. 90, "A sudden end . . ." Emil Ludwig, *Cleopatra* (New York: Viking Press, 1937), 90.

p. 91, "You too my . . ." Ronald Mellor and McGee Marni, *The Ancient Roman World* (New York: Oxford University Press, 2004), 78.

p. 92, "I hate the queen . . ." Grant, *Cleopatra,* 96.

CHAPTER FIVE: The Queen and the General

p. 96, "who owes everything . . ." Brooks, *Goddess of Egypt, Enemy of Rome,* 63.

p. 96-97, "Give them games . . ." Theodore Vrettos, *Alexandria: City of the Western Mind* (New York: The Free Press, 2001), 109.

p. 103, "If you intend . . ." Ibid., 112.

p. 105, "She came sailing . . ." Tom Streissguth, *Queen Cleopatra* (Minneapolis, MN: Lerner Publications, 2000), 7-8.

p. 106, "He found the preparations . . ." Ibid., 62.

p. 106, "Perceiving that his . . ." Weigall, *Life and Times of Cleopatra,* 246.

p. 106-107, "Her beauty . . ." Streissguth, 32.

p. 108, "were very scurvily . . ." Weigall, *Life and Times of Cleopatra,* 263.

p. 109, "Emperor, you had . . ." Hughes-Hallett, *Histories, Dreams, and Distortions,* 72.

CHAPTER SIX: On Her Own

p. 114, "Of domestic mice . . ." Brooks, *Goddess of Egypt, Enemy of Rome,* 79-80.

p. 116, "Words cannot express . . ." Mellor, *The Ancient Roman World,* 68.

CHAPTER SEVEN: Isis and Dionysus Reunited

p. 127, "He that had . . . to their wants" Ludwig, *Cleopatra,* 154.

p.129 , "Is your wife . . ." Brooks, *Goddess of Egypt, Enemy of Rome,* 92.

CHAPTER EIGHT: War With Rome

p. 134, "I do not see . . ." Weigall, *Life and Times of Cleopatra,* 332.

p. 135, "This one island . . ." Streissguth, *Queen Cleopatra,* 80-81.

p. 136, "He gave not . . ." Hughes-Hallett, *Histories, Dreams, and Distortions*, 41.

p.136-137 , "her vile gang . . ." Michel Chaveau, *Cleopatra: Beyond the Myth* (Ithaca, NY: Cornell University Press, 2000), 85.

p. 137-138, "Who would not . . ." Streissguth, *Queen Cleopatra,* 78.

p. 138, "Romans would degenerate . . ." Burstein, *The Reign of Cleopatra*, 66.

p.144 , "Octavian's ships resembled . . ." Streissguth, *Queen Cleopatra*, 89.

CHAPTER NINE: The Snake Strikes

p. 151-152, "The man's inquisitive . . ." Weigall, *Life and Times of Cleopatra*, 399.

p. 152, "might find several . . ." Ibid., 407.

p. 153, "Cleopatra has betrayed . . ." Brooks, *Goddess of Egypt, Enemy of Rome,* 118.

p. 154, "Well done, Eros . . ." Lindsay, *Cleopatra*, 421

p. 154, "fallen not ignobly . . ." Streissguth, *Queen Cleopatra,* 96.

p. 157, "I'll never go . . ." Lindsay, *Cleopatra*, 428.

p. 157, "A fine deed . . . so many kings" Ibid., 432.

p. 160, "Yet she preferred . . ." Brooks, *Goddess of Egypt, Enemy of Rome*, 126.

p. 160, "It is bad . . ." Grant, *Cleopatra*, 229.

p. 163, "There was no . . ." Streissguth, *Queen Cleopatra,* 101-102.

Bibliography

Baines, John, and Málek Jaromir. *Ancient Egypt.* Richmond, VA: Stonehenge Press, 1990.

Brooks, Polly Schoyer. *Cleopatra: Goddess of Egypt, Enemy of Rome.* New York: Harper Collins, 1995.

Burstein, Stanley M. *The Reign of Cleopatra.* Westport, CT: Greenwood Press, 2004.

Chandler, Fiona, Sam Taplin, and Jane Bingham. *The Usborne Internet Linked Encyclopedia of the Roman World.* New York: Scholastic, 2001.

Chauveau, Michel. *Cleopatra: Beyond the Myth.* Translated by David Lorton. Ithaca, NY: Cornell University Press, 2002.

———. *Egypt in the Age of Cleopatra.* Translated by David Lorton. Ithaca, NY: Cornell University Press, 2000.

Chrisp, Peter. *The Roman Empire.* Chicago: World Book
    Inc., 1996.
Cornell, Tim, and John Matthews. *Atlas of the Roman World.*
    New York: Checkman Books, 2002.
Foreman, Laura. *Cleopatra's Palace: In Search of a Legend.*
    New York: Discovery Publishing, 1999.
Fraser, Antonia. *The Warrior Queens.* New York: Vintage
    Books, 1994.
Grant, Michael. *Ancient History Atlas.* New York:
    Macmillan, 1971.
————. *Cleopatra.* London: Phoenix Press, 2000.
————. *History of Rome.* New York: Charles Scribner's
    Sons, 1978.
Green, Robert. *Cleopatra.* New York: Grolier Publishing,
    1996.
Hart, George. *Ancient Egypt.* London: Dorling Kindersley,
    1990.
Hughes-Hallett, Lucy. *Cleopatra: Histories, Dreams, and
    Distortions.* New York: Harper and Row, 1990.
James, Simon. *Ancient Rome.* New York: Alfred A. Knopf,
    1990.
————. *Ancient Rome.* New York: Viking Press, 1992.
Johnson, Paul. *The Civilization of Ancient Rome.* New York:
    Harper Collins, 1999.
Lefkowitz, Mary. *Not Out of Africa.* New York: Basic Books,
    1997.
Lindsay, Jack. *Cleopatra.* New York: Coward McCann &
Geoghegan,
    1970.
Ludwig, Emil. *Cleopatra.* New York: Viking Press, 1937.
Macdonald, Fiona. *Women in Ancient Egypt.* New York: Peter
    Bedrick Books, 1999.

Mellor, Ronald, and McGee Marni. *The Ancient Roman World*. New York: Oxford University Press, 2004.

Morgan, Julian. *Cleopatra: Ruling in the Shadow of Rome*. New York: Rosen Publishing, 2003.

Nardo, Don. *Life in Ancient Rome*. San Diego, CA: Lucent Books, 1997.

Shaw, Ian. *Exploring Ancient Egypt*. New York: Oxford University Press, 2003.

Streissguth, Tom. *Queen Cleopatra*. Minneapolis, MN: Lerner Publications, 2000.

Vrettos, Theodore. *Alexandria: City of the Western Mind*. New York: The Free Press, 2001.

Walker, Susan, and Peter Higgs, eds. *Cleopatra of Egypt: From History to Myth*. Princeton, NJ: Princeton University Press, 2001.

Weigall, Arthur. *The Life and Times of Cleopatra, Queen of Egypt*. New York: G. P. Putnam's Sons/The Knickerbocker Press, 1924.

Weigall, Arthur. *The Life and Times of Marc Antony*. New York: G.P. Putnam's Sons, 1931.

Web sites

http://www.touregypt.net/

Features information on all aspects of Egypt, from detailed histories of the pharaohs to a hieroglyph translator, to tips about visiting Egypt today.

http://www-tech.mit.edu/Shakespeare/cleopatra/full.html

The full text of William Shakespeare's dramatization of Cleopatra's story, *Antony and Cleopatra.*

http://www.davidclaudon.com/Cleo/Cleopatra1.html

A Web site devoted to Cleopatra's depictions on stage and screen, with particular emphasis on what she wore in real life versus the stage interpretations of her costumes. Also features a list of actresses who have played Cleopatra, dating back to the seventeenth century.

http://www.roman-empire.net/

Detailed history, with illustrations, of the Roman Empire. Also features Roman Empire timelines, interactive maps, and sections about Roman religion, dress, and warfare.

Index